T0110677

THE EVANGELIST'S BOOK OF HELPS

Margaret F. Blanchon

Order this book online at www.trafford.com
or email orders@trafford.com

Most Trafford titles are also available at major online book retailers.

© Copyright 2011 Margaret F. Blanchon.
All rights reserved. No part of this publication may be reproduced, stored
in a retrieval system, or transmitted, in any form or by any means, electronic,
mechanical, photocopying, recording, or otherwise, without
the written prior permission of the author.

Printed in the United States of America.

ISBN: 978-1-4269-4711-7 (sc)
ISBN: 978-1-4269-4727-8 (e)

Library of Congress Control Number: 2010941117

Trafford rev. 12/20/2010

 www.trafford.com

North America & international
toll-free: 1 888 232 4444 (USA & Canada)
phone: 250 383 6864 ♦ fax: 812 355 4082

PREFACE

This book enables the Christian evangelist and witness to quickly find the appropriate scripture from the Bible that will pierce the heart of the listener, and bring them to faith in Christ Jesus.

The Person of the Holy Spirit works with His Word, in order to implant Jesus' gift of faith in the hearts of the hearers.

James 1:21
... and receive with meekness the engrafted word, which is able to save your souls.

Colossians 3:16
Let the word of Christ dwell in you richly in all wisdom: teaching and admonishing one another in psalms and hymns and spiritual songs, singing with grace in your hearts to the Lord.

CONTENTS

INTRODUCTION

JESUS UPHOLDS ALL THINGS BY THE WORD OF HIS POWER

JESUS IS THE 'LIVING' WORD OF GOD:

Hebrews 1: 1-3

God … spake in time past unto the fathers by the prophets
Hath in these last days spoken unto us by His Son,
whom He hath appointed Heir of all things,
by whom also He made the worlds;
who being the brightness of His glory,
and the express image of His person,
and upholding all things by the word of His power ..

John 1:1-3

In the beginning was the Word, and the Word was with
God, and the Word was God. The same was in the
beginning with God. All things were made by him; and
without him was not any thing made that was made.

John 1:14

And the Word was made flesh, and dwelt among
us, (and we beheld his glory, the glory as of the only
begotten of the Father,) full of grace and truth.

1 John 1: 1-3

That which was from the beginning, which we have
heard, which we have seen with our eyes, which we

have looked upon, and our hands have handled, of the Word of life;

(For the life was manifested, and we have seen it, and bear witness, and show unto you that eternal life, which was with the Father, and was manifested unto us;)

That which we have seen and heard declare we unto you, that ye also may have fellowship with us: and truly our fellowship is with the Father, and with his Son Jesus Christ.

Revelation 19:11-16

And I saw heaven opened, and behold a white horse; and he that sat upon him was called Faithful and True, and in righteousness he doth judge and make war. His eyes were as a flame of fire, and on his head were many crowns; and he had a name written, that no man knew, but he himself. And he was clothed with a vesture dipped in blood:

and his name is called The Word of God.

And the armies which were in heaven followed him upon white horses, clothed in fine linen, white and clean. And out of his mouth goes a sharp sword, that with it he should smite the nations: and he shall rule them with a rod of iron: and he treads the winepress of the fierceness and wrath of Almighty God. And he has on his vesture and on his thigh a name written,

KING OF KINGS, AND LORD OF LORDS.

THE PERSON OF THE HOLY SPIRIT – HE IS THE POWER OF GOD

Micah 3:8
> But truly I am full of power by the Spirit of the Lord

Romans 8:11
> But if the Spirit of Him that raised up Jesus from the dead dwell in you, He that raised up Christ from the dead shall also quicken your mortal bodies by His Spirit that dwells in you.

THE SWORD OF THE HOLY SPIRIT IS THE WRITTEN WORD OF GOD

Ephesians 6:17
> … and the Sword of the Spirit which is the word of God ..

When we, as Holy Spirit-filled believers, speak the word of God – the scriptures from the Bible –in our prayers, or in witnessing and proclaiming the gospel, the Holy Spirit empowers/ anoints His word to manifest in our lives, and in the hearts of the hearers.

Acts 4:29-31
> And now, Lord, behold their threatenings; and grant unto thy servants, that with all boldness they may speak Thy word, by stretching forth Thine hand to heal; and

that signs and wonders may be done by the name of thy holy child Jesus.

And when they had prayed, the place was shaken where they were assembled together; and they were all filled with the Holy Ghost, and they spoke the word of God with boldness.

Romans 10:17

Faith comes by hearing, and hearing by the word of God.

Hebrews 4:12

For the word of God is quick and powerful and sharper than any two-edged sword, piercing even to the dividing asunder of soul and spirit, and of the joints and marrow, and is a discerner of the thoughts and intents of the heart.

THE BIBLE IS THE WRITTEN WORD OF GOD

Deuteronomy 8:3

… man doth not live by bread only, but by every word that proceedeth out of the mouth of the LORD doth man live.

Isaiah 55:11

So shall my word be that goeth forth out of my mouth: it shall not return unto me void, but it shall accomplish that which I please, and it shall prosper in the thing whereto I sent it.

Psalm 68:11

The LORD gave the word: great was the company of those that published it.

Psalm 119:30

The entrance of Thy words gives light; it gives understanding unto the simple.

Psalm 119:89

Forever, O Lord, thy word is settled in heaven

Psalm 119:105

Thy word is a lamp unto my feet, and a light unto my path

2 Timothy 3:16

All scripture is given by inspiration of God ...

Hebrews 1:1

God, who at sundry times and in divers manners, spoke in times past unto the fathers by the prophets, has, in these last days spoken unto us by His Son, whom He has appointed heir of all things, by whom also He made the worlds

2 Peter 1:21

For the prophecy came not in old time by the will of men; but holy men of God spoke as they were moved by the Holy Ghost.

The following scriptures are given under the various headings, to enable the Christian witness and evangelist to be more effective.

All scripture references in this book are taken from:
The King James Bible (Authorized Version)

THE BIBLE IS THE WORD OF GOD

Psalm 119:89
> For ever, O LORD, thy word is settled in heaven.

Psalm 119:105
> Thy word is a lamp unto my feet, and a light unto my path.

Psalm 119: 130
> The entrance of thy words giveth light; it giveth understanding unto the simple.

Job 23:12
> I have esteemed the words of his mouth more than my necessary food.

Jeremiah 23:29
> Is not my word like as a fire? says the LORD; and like a hammer that breaks the rock in pieces?

Luke 18:31
> Then he took unto him the twelve, and said unto them, Behold, we go up to Jerusalem, and all things that are written by the prophets concerning the Son of man shall be accomplished.

Acts 10:43

To him give all the prophets witness, that through his name whosoever believeth in him shall receive remission of sins.

2 Peter 1:16-21

For we have not followed cunningly devised fables, when we made known unto you the power and coming of our Lord Jesus Christ, but were eyewitnesses of his majesty.

For he received from God the Father honour and glory, when there came such a voice to him from the excellent glory, This is my beloved Son, in whom I am well pleased. And this voice which came from heaven we heard, when we were with him in the holy mount.

We have also a more sure word of prophecy; whereunto ye do well that ye take heed, as unto a light that shineth in a dark place, until the day dawn, and the day star arise in your hearts: Knowing this first, that no prophecy of the scripture is of any private interpretation. For the prophecy came not in old time by the will of man: but holy men of God spoke as they were moved by the Holy Ghost.

JESUS IS THE LIVING WORD OF GOD

John 1:1-4

In the beginning was the Word, and the Word was with God, and the Word was God.

The same was in the beginning with God.

All things were made by him; and without him was not any thing made that was made.

In him was life; and the life was the light of men.

John 1:14

And the Word was made flesh, and dwelt among us, (and we beheld his glory, the glory as of the only begotten of the Father,) full of grace and truth.

Hebrews 1:1-3

God, who at sundry times and in divers manners spake in time past unto the fathers by the prophets,

Hath in these last days spoken unto us by his Son, whom he hath appointed heir of all things, by whom also he made the worlds;

Who being the brightness of his glory, and the express image of his person, and upholding all things by the word of his power, when he had by himself purged our sins, sat down on the right hand of the Majesty on high:

1 John 1:1-3

That which was from the beginning, which we have heard, which we have seen with our eyes, which we have looked upon, and our hands have handled, of the Word of life;

(For the life was manifested, and we have seen it, and bear witness, and shew unto you that eternal life, which was with the Father, and was manifested unto us;)

That which we have seen and heard declare we unto you, that ye also may have fellowship with us: and truly our fellowship is with the Father, and with his Son Jesus Christ.

Revelation 19:13-16

And he was clothed with a vesture dipped in blood: and his name is called The Word of God. And the armies which were in heaven followed him upon white horses, clothed in fine linen, white and clean. And out of his mouth goes a sharp sword, that with it he should smite the nations: and he shall rule them with a rod of iron: and he treads the winepress of the fierceness and wrath of Almighty God. And he hath on his vesture and on his thigh a name written, KING OF KINGS, AND LORD OF LORDS.

JESUS CHRIST IS GOD THE SON

Psalm 110:1

The LORD said unto my Lord, Sit thou at my right hand, until I make thine enemies thy footstool.

Luke 20:42,43

David himself saith in the book of Psalms, The LORD said unto my Lord, Sit thou on my right hand, Till I make thine enemies thy footstool.

Proverbs 8:22-36

The LORD possessed me in the beginning of his way, before his works of old.

I was set up from everlasting, from the beginning, or ever the earth was.

When there were no depths, I was brought forth; when there were no fountains abounding with water.

Before the mountains were settled, before the hills was I brought forth:

While as yet he had not made the earth, nor the fields, nor the highest part of the dust of the world.

When he prepared the heavens, I was there: when he set a compass upon the face of the depth:

When he established the clouds above: when he strengthened the fountains of the deep:

When he gave to the sea his decree, that the waters should not pass his commandment: when he appointed the foundations of the earth:

Then I was by him, as one brought up with him: and I was daily his delight, rejoicing always before him;

Rejoicing in the habitable part of his earth; and my delights were with the sons of men.

Now therefore hearken unto me, O ye children: for blessed are they that keep my ways.

Hear instruction, and be wise, and refuse it not.

Blessed is the man that heareth me, watching daily at my gates, waiting at the posts of my doors.

For whoso findeth me findeth life, and shall obtain favour of the LORD.

But he that sinneth against me wrongeth his own soul: all they that hate me love death.

Isaiah 7:14

Therefore the Lord himself shall give you a sign; Behold, a virgin shall conceive, and bear a son, and shall call his name Immanuel.

Isaiah 9:6

For unto us a child is born, unto us a son is given: and the government shall be upon his shoulder: and his name shall be called Wonderful, Counsellor,

The mighty God, The everlasting Father, The Prince
of Peace.

Isaiah 48:16

Come ye near unto me, hear ye this; I have not
spoken in secret from the beginning; from the time
that it was, there am I: and now the Lord GOD,
and his Spirit, hath sent me.

Matthew 1:21-23

And she shall bring forth a son, and thou shalt call
his name JESUS: for he shall save his people from
their sins.

Now all this was done, that it might be fulfilled
which was spoken of the Lord by the prophet,
saying,

Behold, a virgin shall be with child, and shall bring
forth a son, and they shall call his name Emmanuel,
which being interpreted is, God with us.

Matthew 3:16

And Jesus, when he was baptized, went up
straightway out of the water: and, lo, the heavens
were opened unto him, and he saw the Spirit of God
descending like a dove, and lighting upon him:

Matthew 10:32

Whosoever therefore shall confess me before men,
him will I confess also before my Father which is
in heaven.

Matthew 16:16

And Simon Peter answered and said, Thou art the Christ, the Son of the living God.

Matthew 17:5

While he yet spake, behold, a bright cloud overshadowed them: and behold a voice out of the cloud, which said, This is my beloved Son, in whom I am well pleased; hear ye him.

Matthew 28:18-20

And Jesus came and spake unto them, saying, All power is given unto me in heaven and in earth.

Go ye therefore, and teach all nations, baptizing them in the name of the Father, and of the Son, and of the Holy Ghost:

Teaching them to observe all things whatsoever I have commanded you: and, lo, I am with you always, even unto the end of the world. Amen.

Mark 1:11

And there came a voice from heaven, saying, Thou art my beloved Son, in whom I am well pleased.

Luke 1:35

And the angel answered and said unto her, The Holy Ghost shall come upon thee, and the power of the Highest shall overshadow thee: therefore also that holy thing which shall be born of thee shall be called the Son of God.

Luke 4:41

And devils also came out of many, crying out, and saying, Thou art Christ the Son of God. And he rebuking them suffered them not to speak: for they knew that he was Christ.

Luke 9:35

And there came a voice out of the cloud, saying, This is my beloved Son: hear him.

John 1:14

And the Word was made flesh, and dwelt among us, (and we beheld his glory, the glory as of the only begotten of the Father,) full of grace and truth.

John 1:34

And I saw, and bare record that this is the Son of God.

John 3:16

For God so loved the world, that he gave his only begotten Son, that whosoever believeth in him should not perish, but have everlasting life.

John 3:35

The Father loveth the Son, and hath given all things into his hand.

John 5:21-23

That all men should honour the Son, even as they honour the Father. He that honoureth not the Son honoureth not the Father which hath sent him.

John 8:23

> *And he said unto them, Ye are from beneath; I am from above: ye are of this world; I am not of this world.*

John 9:35-38

> *Jesus heard that they had cast him out; and when he had found him, he said unto him, Dost thou believe on the Son of God?*

John 10:30

> *I and my Father are one.*

John 11:27

> *She saith unto him, Yea, Lord: I believe that thou art the Christ, the Son of God, which should come into the world.*

John 14:11,13

> *Believe me that I am in the Father, and the Father in me: or else believe me for the very works' sake.*
>
> *And whatsoever ye shall ask in my name, that will I do, that the Father may be glorified in the Son.*

John 14:6

> *Jesus saith unto him, I am the way, the truth, and the life: no man cometh unto the Father, but by me.*

John 16:28

> *I came forth from the Father, and am come into the world: again, I leave the world, and go to the Father.*

John 17:1-5

These words spake Jesus, and lifted up his eyes to heaven, and said, Father, the hour is come; glorify thy Son, that thy Son also may glorify thee:

As thou hast given him power over all flesh, that he should give eternal life to as many as thou hast given him.

And this is life eternal, that they might know thee the only true God, and Jesus Christ, whom thou hast sent.

I have glorified thee on the earth: I have finished the work which thou gavest me to do.

And now, O Father, glorify thou me with thine own self with the glory which I had with thee before the world was.

John 20:31

But these are written, that ye might believe that Jesus is the Christ, the Son of God; and that believing ye might have life through his name.

Acts 8:37

And Philip said, If thou believest with all thine heart, thou mayest. And he answered and said, I believe that Jesus Christ is the Son of God.

Romans 15:6

That ye may with one mind and one mouth glorify God, even the Father of our Lord Jesus Christ.

Philippians 2:9-11

Wherefore God also hath highly exalted him, and given him a name which is above every name:

That at the name of Jesus every knee should bow, of things in heaven, and things in earth, and things under the earth;

And that every tongue should confess that Jesus Christ is Lord, to the glory of God the Father.

Colossians 1:13,14
Who hath delivered us from the power of darkness, and hath translated us into the kingdom of his dear Son: In whom we have redemption through his blood, even the forgiveness of sins:

Colossians 2:9
For in him dwelleth all the fulness of the Godhead bodily.

1 Thessalonians 1:10
And to wait for his Son from heaven, whom he raised from the dead, even Jesus, which delivered us from the wrath to come.

Hebrews 1:1-3
God, who at sundry times and in divers manners spake in time past unto the fathers by the prophets,

Hath in these last days spoken unto us by his Son, whom he hath appointed heir of all things, by whom also he made the worlds;

Who being the brightness of his glory, and the express image of his person, and upholding all things by the word of his power, when he had by himself purged our sins, sat down on the right hand of the Majesty on high:

2 Peter 1:17

For he received from God the Father honour and glory, when there came such a voice to him from the excellent glory, This is my beloved Son, in whom I am well pleased.

1 John 1:3

That which we have seen and heard declare we unto you, that ye also may have fellowship with us: and truly our fellowship is with the Father, and with his Son Jesus Christ

1 John 3:8

He that committeth sin is of the devil; for the devil sinneth from the beginning. For this purpose the Son of God was manifested, that he might destroy the works of the devil.

1 John 4:9

In this was manifested the love of God toward us, because that God sent his only begotten Son into the world, that we might live through him.

1 John 4:14,15

And we have seen and do testify that the Father sent the Son to be the Saviour of the world.

Whosoever shall confess that Jesus is the Son of God, God dwelleth in him, and he in God.

1 John 5:5

Who is he that overcometh the world, but he that believeth that Jesus is the Son of God?

1 John 5:11,12,13

And this is the record, that God hath given to us eternal life, and this life is in his Son.

He that hath the Son hath life; and he that hath not the Son of God hath not life.

These things have I written unto you that believe on the name of the Son of God; that ye may know that ye have eternal life, and that ye may believe on the name of the Son of God.

2 John 1:9

Whosoever transgresseth, and abideth not in the doctrine of Christ, hath not God. He that abideth in the doctrine of Christ, he hath both the Father and the Son.

Revelation 3:5

He that overcometh, the same shall be clothed in white raiment; and I will not blot out his name out of the book of life, but I will confess his name before my Father, and before his angels.

THE DEITY OF JESUS CHRIST

**The New Testament clearly presents Jesus Christ as God.
The word 'Jesus' means - 'GOD SAVES'.
The word 'Christ' means - 'THE ANOINTED ONE'.**

Isaiah 45:21-23

Tell ye, and bring them near; yea, let them take counsel together: who hath declared this from ancient time? who hath told it from that time? have not I the LORD? and there is no God else beside me; a just God and a Saviour; there is none beside me.

Look unto me, and be ye saved, all the ends of the earth: for I am God, and there is none else.

I have sworn by myself, the word is gone out of my mouth in righteousness, and shall not return, That unto me every knee shall bow, every tongue shall swear.

Isaiah 7:14 / Matthew 1:23

Therefore the Lord himself shall give you a sign; Behold, a virgin shall conceive, and bear a son, and shall call his name Immanuel

Matthew 1:23

Behold, a virgin shall be with child, and shall bring forth a son, and they shall call his name Emmanuel, which being interpreted is, God with us.

John 1:1-3

In the beginning was the Word, and the Word was with God, and the Word was God.

The same was in the beginning with God.

All things were made by him; and without him was not any thing made that was made.

Romans 9:5

Whose are the fathers, and of whom as concerning the flesh Christ came, who is over all, God blessed for ever. Amen.

Colossians 1: 13-22

Who hath delivered us from the power of darkness, and hath translated us into the kingdom of his dear Son:In whom we have redemption through his blood, even the forgiveness of sins:

Who is the image of the invisible God, the firstborn of every creature:

For by him were all things created, that are in heaven, and that are in earth, visible and invisible, whether they be thrones, or dominions, or principalities, or powers: all things were created by him, and for him:

And he is before all things, and by him all things consist.

And he is the head of the body, the church: who is the beginning, the firstborn from the dead; that in all things he might have the preeminence.

For it pleased the Father that in him should all fullness dwell;

And, having made peace through the blood of his cross, by him to reconcile all things unto himself; by him, I say, whether they be things in earth, or things in heaven.

And you, that were sometime alienated and enemies in your mind by wicked works, yet now hath he reconciled

In the body of his flesh through death, to present you holy and unblameable and unreproveable in his sight:

Colossians 2:9

For in him dwelleth all the fulness of the Godhead bodily.

Hebrews 1:1-8

God, who at sundry times and in divers manners spake in time past unto the fathers by the prophets,

Hath in these last days spoken unto us by his Son, whom he hath appointed heir of all things, by whom also he made the worlds;

Who being the brightness of his glory, and the express image of his person, and upholding all things by the word of his power, when he had by himself purged our sins, sat down on the right hand of the Majesty on high:

Being made so much better than the angels, as he hath by inheritance obtained a more excellent name than they.

For unto which of the angels said he at any time, Thou art my Son, this day have I begotten thee? And again, I will be to him a Father, and he shall be to me a Son?

And again, when he bringeth in the first begotten into the world, he saith, And let all the angels of God worship him.

And of the angels he saith, Who maketh his angels spirits, and his ministers a flame of fire.

But unto the Son he saith, Thy throne, O God, is for ever and ever: a sceptre of righteousness is the sceptre of thy kingdom.

Titus 2:13

Looking for that blessed hope, and the glorious appearing of the great God and our Saviour Jesus Christ;

1 John 5:20,21

And we know that the Son of God is come, and hath given us an understanding, that we may know him that is true, and we are in him that is true, even in his Son Jesus Christ. This is the true God, and eternal life.

JESUS IS SELF-EXISTENT

John 1:4

In Him was life; and the life was the light of men.

John 5:11

> *And this is the record, that God has given to us eternal life, and this life is in His Son.*

John 14:6

> *Jesus said unto him, I am the way, the truth and the life: no man comes unto the Father, but by Me.*

JESUS IS OMNIPRESENT: ALWAYS PRESENT

Matthew 18:20

> *For where two or three are gathered together in My name, Here am I in the midst.*

Matthew 28:20

> *… and lo, I am with you always, even unto the end of the world. Amen.*

John 8:58

> *Before Abraham was, I AM.*

Exodus 3:14

> *And God said unto Moses, I AM THAT I AM: and he said, Thus shalt thou say unto the children of Israel, I AM hath sent me unto you.*

John 17:5

> *And now O Father, glorify Thou Me with Thine own self with the glory which I had with Thee before the world was.*

Hebrews 13:5
> .. I will never leave thee, nor forsake thee.

JESUS IS OMNISCIENT – ALL-KNOWING

Matthew 17:22-27
> And while they abode in Galilee, Jesus said unto them, The Son of man shall be betrayed into the hands of men: and they shall kill Him, and the third day He shall rise again.

John 4:18
> For you have had five husbands, and he whom you now have is not your husband.

John 6:64
> But there are some of you that believe not. For Jesus knew from the beginning who they were that believed not, and who should betray Him.

JESUS IS OMNIPOTENT – ALL POWERFUL

Matthew 8:26,27
> And he saith unto them, Why are ye fearful, O ye of little faith? Then he arose, and rebuked the winds and the sea; and there was a great calm.

> But the men marvelled, saying, What manner of man is this, that even the winds and the sea obey him!

Mark 6:48

> *And he saw them toiling in rowing; for the wind was contrary unto them: and about the fourth watch of the night he cometh unto them, walking upon the sea, and would have passed by them.*

Luke 4:39-41

> *And he stood over her, and rebuked the fever; and it left her: and immediately she arose and ministered unto them.*

> *Now when the sun was setting, all they that had any sick with divers diseases brought them unto him; and he laid his hands on every one of them, and healed them. And devils also came out of many, crying out, and saying, Thou art Christ the Son of God. And he rebuking them suffered them not to speak: for they knew that he was Christ.*

Luke 7:14

> *And he came and touched the bier: and they that bare him stood still. And he said, Young man, I say unto thee, Arise.*

Revelation 1:8

> *I am Alpha and Omega, the beginning and the ending, saith the Lord, which is, and which was, and which is to come, the Almighty.*

Revelation 19:13-16

> *And he was clothed with a vesture dipped in blood: and his name is called The Word of God.*

And the armies which were in heaven followed him upon white horses, clothed in fine linen, white and clean.

And out of his mouth goeth a sharp sword, that with it he should smite the nations: and he shall rule them with a rod of iron: and he treadeth the winepress of the fierceness and wrath of Almighty God.

And he hath on his vesture and on his thigh a name written, KING OF KINGS, AND LORD OF LORDS.

JESUS IS OUR ETERNAL LIFE

John 1:4
In Him was life, and the life was the light of men.

1 John 5:11,12
And this is the record, that God has given to us eternal life, and this life is in His Son. He that has the Son has life, he that has not the Son of God has not life.

BY JESUS CHRIST WERE ALL THINGS CREATED

John 1:1

In the beginning was the Word, and the Word was with God, and the Word was God. The same was in the beginning with God. All things were made by Him; and without Him was not anything made that was made. In Him was life; and the life was the light of men.

John 3: 35,36

The Father loveth the Son, and hath given all things into his hand.

He that believeth on the Son hath everlasting life: and he that believeth not the Son shall not see life; but the wrath of God abideth on him.

Ephesians 3:9

And to make all men see what is the fellowship of the mystery, which from the beginning of the world hath been hid in God, who created all things by Jesus Christ:

Margaret F. Blanchon

Colossians 1: 13-19

Who hath delivered us from the power of darkness, and hath translated us into the kingdom of his dear Son:

In whom we have redemption through his blood, even the forgiveness of sins:

Who is the image of the invisible God, the firstborn of every creature:

For by him were all things created, that are in heaven, and that are in earth, visible and invisible, whether they be thrones, or dominions, or principalities, or powers: all things were created by him, and for him:

And he is before all things, and by him all things consist.

And he is the head of the body, the church: who is the beginning, the firstborn from the dead; that in all things he might have the preeminence.

For it pleased the Father that in him should all fulness dwell;

Hebrews 1: 2-10

Hath in these last days spoken unto us by his Son, whom he hath appointed heir of all things, by whom also he made the worlds;

Who being the brightness of his glory, and the express image of his person, and upholding all things by the word of his power, when he had by himself purged our sins, sat down on the right hand of the Majesty on high:

Being made so much better than the angels, as he hath by inheritance obtained a more excellent name than they.

For unto which of the angels said he at any time, Thou art my Son, this day have I begotten thee? And again, I will be to him a Father, and he shall be to me a Son?

And again, when he bringeth in the first begotten into the world, he saith, And let all the angels of God worship him.

And of the angels he saith, Who maketh his angels spirits, and his ministers a flame of fire.

But unto the Son he saith, Thy throne, O God, is for ever and ever: a sceptre of righteousness is the sceptre of thy kingdom.

Thou hast loved righteousness, and hated iniquity; therefore God, even thy God, hath anointed thee with the oil of gladness above thy fellows.

And, Thou, Lord, in the beginning hast laid the foundation of the earth; and the heavens are the works of thine hands:

THE PRE-EXISTENCE OF JESUS CHRIST

JESUS EXISTED BEFORE THE FOUNDATION OF THE WORLD

Exodus 3:14

And God said unto Moses, I AM THAT I AM: and he said, Thus shalt thou say unto the children of Israel, I AM hath sent me unto you.

John 1:1

In the beginning was the Word, and the Word was with God, and the Word was God; the same was in the beginning with God.

John 1:14

The Word was made flesh and dwelt among us ..

John 3:31

He that cometh from above is above all: he that is of the earth is earthly, and speaketh of the earth: he that cometh from heaven is above all.

John 8:58

Before Abraham was, I AM.

JESUS WAS BEFORE ALL THINGS –
BEFORE THE STARS AND BEFORE THE UNIVERSE

Proverbs 8:22

The LORD possessed me in the beginning of his way, before his works of old.

John 3:31

He that comes from above is above all: he that is of the earth is earthly, and speaks of the earth: He that comes from heaven is above all.

Colossians 1:17

And he is before all things, and by him all things consist.

1 Peter 1:20

Who verily was ordained before the foundation of the world, but was manifest in these last times for you.

Revelation 1:8

I am Alpha and Omega, the beginning and the ending, saith the Lord, which is, and which was, and which is to come, the Almighty.

JESUS CHRIST IS KING OF KINGS AND LORD OF LORDS

Isaiah 9:6

For unto us a child is born, unto us a son is given: and the government shall be upon his shoulder: and his name shall be called Wonderful, Counsellor, The mighty God, The everlasting Father, The Prince of Peace.

Zechariah 14:16

And it shall come to pass, that every one that is left of all the nations which came against Jerusalem shall even go up from year to year to worship the King, the LORD of hosts, and to keep the feast of tabernacles.

Matthew 7:21

Not every one that saith unto me, Lord, Lord, shall enter into the kingdom of heaven; but he that doeth the will of my Father which is in heaven.

Luke 2:11

For unto you is born this day in the city of David a Saviour, which is Christ the Lord.

Romans 14:11

For it is written, As I live, saith the Lord, every knee shall bow to me, and every tongue shall confess to God.

Philippians 2:10,11

That at the name of Jesus every knee should bow, of things in heaven, and things in earth, and things under the earth; And that every tongue should confess that Jesus Christ is Lord, to the glory of God the Father.

Colossians 1:13-22

Who hath delivered us from the power of darkness, and hath translated us into the kingdom of his dear Son:

In whom we have redemption through his blood, even the forgiveness of sins:

Who is the image of the invisible God, the firstborn of every creature:

For by him were all things created, that are in heaven, and that are in earth, visible and invisible, whether they be thrones, or dominions, or principalities, or powers: all things were created by him, and for him:

And he is before all things, and by him all things consist.

And he is the head of the body, the church: who is the beginning, the firstborn from the dead; that in all things he might have the preeminence.

For it pleased the Father that in him should all fulness dwell;

And, having made peace through the blood of his cross, by him to reconcile all things unto himself; by him, I say, whether they be things in earth, or things in heaven.

And you, that were sometime alienated and enemies in your mind by wicked works, yet now hath he reconciled in the body of his flesh through death, to present you holy and unblameable and unreproveable in his sight:

Revelation 1:8

I am Alpha and Omega, the beginning and the ending, saith the Lord, which is, and which was, and which is to come, the Almighty.

Revelation 3:5

He that overcometh, the same shall be clothed in white raiment; and I will not blot out his name out of the book of life, but I will confess his name before my Father, and before his angels.

Revelation 19:11-16

And I saw heaven opened, and behold a white horse; and he that sat upon him was called Faithful and True, and in righteousness he doth judge and make war.

His eyes were as a flame of fire, and on his head were many crowns; and he had a name written, that no man knew, but he himself.

And he was clothed with a vesture dipped in blood: and his name is called The Word of God.

And the armies which were in heaven followed him upon white horses, clothed in fine linen, white and clean.

And out of his mouth goeth a sharp sword, that with it he should smite the nations: and he shall rule them with a rod of iron: and he treadeth the winepress of the fierceness and wrath of Almighty God.

And he hath on his vesture and on his thigh a name written, KING OF KINGS, AND LORD OF LORDS.

LORD JESUS CHRIST'S VIRGIN BIRTH

Matthew 1: 18-23

Now the birth of Jesus Christ was on this wise: When as his mother Mary was espoused to Joseph, before they came together, she was found with child of the Holy Ghost.

Then Joseph her husband, being a just man, and not willing to make her a public example, was minded to put her away privily.

But while he thought on these things, behold, the angel of the LORD appeared unto him in a dream, saying, Joseph, thou son of David, fear not to take unto thee Mary thy wife: for that which is conceived in her is of the Holy Ghost.

And she shall bring forth a son, and thou shalt call his name JESUS: for he shall save his people from their sins.

Now all this was done, that it might be fulfilled which was spoken of the Lord by the prophet, saying,

Behold, a virgin shall be with child, and shall bring forth a son, and they shall call his name Emmanuel, which being interpreted is, God with us.

Isaiah 7:14

> *Therefore the Lord himself shall give you a sign; Behold, a virgin shall conceive, and bear a son, and shall call his name Immanuel.*

Luke 1:30-35

> *And the angel said unto her, Fear not, Mary: for thou hast found favour with God.*

> *And, behold, thou shalt conceive in thy womb, and bring forth a son, and shalt call his name JESUS.*

> *He shall be great, and shall be called the Son of the Highest: and the Lord God shall give unto him the throne of his father David:*

> *And he shall reign over the house of Jacob for ever; and of his kingdom there shall be no end.*

> *Then said Mary unto the angel, How shall this be, seeing I know not a man?*

> *And the angel answered and said unto her, The Holy Ghost shall come upon thee, and the power of the Highest shall overshadow thee: therefore*

> *also that holy thing which shall be born of thee shall be called the Son of God.*

Luke 2:8-14

> *And there were in the same country shepherds abiding in the field, keeping watch over their flock by night.*

> *And, lo, the angel of the Lord came upon them, and the glory of the Lord shone round about them: and they were sore afraid.*

And the angel said unto them, Fear not: for, behold, I bring you good tidings of great joy, which shall be to all people.

For unto you is born this day in the city of David a Saviour, which is Christ the Lord.

And this shall be a sign unto you; Ye shall find the babe wrapped in swaddling clothes, lying in a manger.

And suddenly there was with the angel a multitude of the heavenly host praising God, and saying,

Glory to God in the highest, and on earth peace, good will toward men.

LORD JESUS CHRIST'S DEATH

Psalm 22:16

For dogs have compassed me: the assembly of the wicked have inclosed me: they pierced my hands and my feet.

Isaiah 53:10-12

Yet it pleased the LORD to bruise him; he hath put him to grief: when thou shalt make his soul an offering for sin, he shall see his seed, he shall prolong his days, and the pleasure of the LORD shall prosper in his hand.

He shall see of the travail of his soul, and shall be satisfied: by his knowledge shall my righteous servant justify many; for he shall bear their iniquities.

Therefore will I divide him a portion with the great, and he shall divide the spoil with the strong; because he hath poured out his soul unto death: and he was numbered with the transgressors; and he bare the sin of many, and made intercession for the transgressors.

Isaiah 53:55

But he was wounded for our transgressions, he was bruised for our iniquities: the chastisement of our peace was upon him; and with his stripes we are healed.

Zechariah 11:12

And I said unto them, If ye think good, give me my price; and if not, forbear. So they weighed for my price thirty pieces of silver.

Zechariah 12:10

And I will pour upon the house of David, and upon the inhabitants of Jerusalem, the spirit of grace and of supplications: and they shall look upon me whom they have pierced, and they shall mourn for him, as one mourneth for his only son, and shall be in bitterness for him, as one that is in bitterness for his firstborn.

Matthew 20:28

Just as the Son of Man did not come to be served, but to serve, and to give his life as a ransom for many.

Mark 10:45

For even the Son of man came not to be ministered unto, but to minister, and to give his life a ransom for many.

Luke 24:46

And said unto them, Thus it is written, and thus it behooved Christ to suffer, and to rise from the dead the third day:

John 1:29

The next day John seeth Jesus coming unto him, and saith, Behold the Lamb of God, which taketh away the sin of the world.

John 3:14

> *And as Moses lifted up the serpent in the wilderness, even so must the Son of man be lifted up:*

John 6:51

> *I am the living bread which came down from heaven: if any man eat of this bread, he shall live for ever: and the bread that I will give is my flesh, which I will give for the life of the world.*

John 10:15

> *As the Father knoweth me, even so know I the Father: and I lay down my life for the sheep.*

John 11:49-52

> *And one of them, named Caiaphas, being the high priest that same year, said unto them, Ye know nothing at all,*
>
> *Nor consider that it is expedient for us, that one man should die for the people, and that the whole nation perish not.*
>
> *And this spake he not of himself: but being high priest that year, he prophesied that Jesus should die for that nation;*
>
> *And not for that nation only, but that also he should gather together in one the children of God that were scattered abroad.*

John 12:32

> *And I, if I be lifted up from the earth, will draw all men unto me.*

John 15:13

Greater love hath no man than this, that a man lay down his life for his friends.

Acts 2:23-27

Him, being delivered by the determinate counsel and foreknowledge of God, ye have taken, and by wicked hands have crucified and slain:

Whom God hath raised up, having loosed the pains of death: because it was not possible that he should be holden of it.

For David speaketh concerning him, I foresaw the Lord always before my face, for he is on my right hand, that I should not be moved:

Therefore did my heart rejoice, and my tongue was glad; moreover also my flesh shall rest in hope:

Because thou wilt not leave my soul in hell, neither wilt thou suffer thine Holy One to see corruption.

Romans 5:8-11

But God commendeth his love toward us, in that, while we were yet sinners, Christ died for us. Much more then, being now justified by his blood, we shall be saved from wrath through him. For if, when we were enemies, we were reconciled to God by the death of his Son, much more, being reconciled, we shall be saved by his life

And not only so, but we also joy in God through our Lord Jesus Christ, by whom we have now received the atonement.

Romans 8:32

He that spared not his own Son, but delivered him up for us all, how shall he not with him also freely give us all things?

2 Corinthians 5:18-21

And all things are of God, who hath reconciled us to himself by Jesus Christ, and hath given to us the ministry of reconciliation;

To wit, that God was in Christ, reconciling the world unto himself, not imputing their trespasses unto them; and hath committed unto us the word of reconciliation.

Now then we are ambassadors for Christ, as though God did beseech you by us: we pray you in Christ's stead, be ye reconciled to God.

For he hath made him to be sin for us, who knew no sin; that we might be made the righteousness of God in him.

Galatians 1:4

Who gave himself for our sins, that he might deliver us from this present evil world, according to the will of God and our Father:

Galatians 2:20

I am crucified with Christ: nevertheless I live; yet not I, but Christ liveth in me: and the life which I now live in the flesh I live by the faith of the Son of God, who loved me, and gave himself for me.

Ephesians 5:2

And walk in love, as Christ also hath loved us, and hath given Himself for us an offering and a sacrifice to God for a sweet smelling savour.

Philippians 2:8

And being found in fashion as a man, he humbled himself, and became obedient unto death, even the death of the cross.

1 Timothy 2:5,6

For there is one God, and one mediator between God and men, the man Christ Jesus; Who gave himself a ransom for all, to be testified in due time.

1 Timothy 3:16

And without controversy great is the mystery of godliness: God was manifest in the flesh, justified in the Spirit, seen of angels, preached unto the Gentiles, believed on in the world, received up into glory.

Titus 2:13,14

Looking for that blessed hope, and the glorious appearing of the great God and our Saviour Jesus Christ; Who gave himself for us, that he might redeem us from all iniquity, and purify unto himself a peculiar people, zealous of good works.

Hebrews 1:1-3

God, who at sundry times and in divers manners spake in time past unto the fathers by the prophets,

Hath in these last days spoken unto us by his Son, whom he hath appointed heir of all things, by whom also he made the worlds;

Who being the brightness of his glory, and the express image of his person, and upholding all things by the word of his power, when he had by himself purged our sins, sat down on the right hand of the Majesty on high:

Hebrews 2:9

But we see Jesus, who was made a little lower than the angels for the suffering of death, crowned with glory and honour; that he by the grace of God should taste death for every man.

Hebrews 2:14

Forasmuch then as the children are partakers of flesh and blood, he also himself likewise took part of the same; that through death he might destroy him that had the power of death, that is, the devil;

Hebrews 9:26-28

For then must he often have suffered since the foundation of the world: but now once in the end of the world hath he appeared to put away sin by the sacrifice of himself.

And as it is appointed unto men once to die, but after this the judgment:

So Christ was once offered to bear the sins of many; and unto them that look for him shall he appear the second time without sin unto salvation.

Hebrews 10:5-7

Wherefore when he cometh into the world, he saith, Sacrifice and offering thou wouldest not, but a body hast thou prepared me:

In burnt offerings and sacrifices for sin thou hast had no pleasure.

Then said I, Lo, I come (in the volume of the book it is written of me,) to do thy will, O God.

Hebrews 10:12

But this man, after he had offered one sacrifice for sins for ever, sat down on the right hand of God;

1 Peter 2:24

Who his own self bare our sins in his own body on the tree, that we, being dead to sins, should live unto righteousness: by whose stripes ye were healed.

1 Peter 3:18

For Christ also hath once suffered for sins, the just for the unjust, that he might bring us to God, being put to death in the flesh, but quickened by the Spirit:

LORD JESUS CHRIST IS THE RESURRECTION AND THE LIFE

Matthew 28:18-20

And Jesus came and spake unto them, saying, All power is given unto me in heaven and in earth.

Go ye therefore, and teach all nations, baptizing them in the name of the Father, and of the Son, and of the Holy Ghost:

Teaching them to observe all things whatsoever I have commanded you: and, lo, I am with you always, even unto the end of the world. Amen.

Luke 13:32

And he said unto them, Go ye, and tell that fox, Behold, I cast out devils, and I do cures to day and to morrow, and the third day I shall be perfected.

Luke 16:31

And he said unto him, If they hear not Moses and the prophets, neither will they be persuaded, though one rose from the dead

Luke 24:44-47

And he said unto them, These are the words which I spake unto you, while I was yet with you, that all things must be fulfilled, which were written in the law of Moses, and in the prophets, and in the psalms, concerning me.

Then opened he their understanding, that they might understand the scriptures,

And said unto them, Thus it is written, and thus it behooved Christ to suffer, and to rise from the dead the third day:

And that repentance and remission of sins should be preached in his name among all nations, beginning at Jerusalem.

Luke 24:27

And beginning at Moses and all the prophets, he expounded unto them in all the scriptures the things concerning himself.

Luke 24:32

And they said one to another, Did not our heart burn within us, while he talked with us by the way, and while he opened to us the scriptures?

John 8:51

Verily, verily, I say unto you, If a man keep my saying, he shall never see death.

John 10:28

And I give unto them eternal life; and they shall never perish, neither shall any man pluck them out of my hand.

John 11: 25,26

Jesus said unto her, I am the resurrection, and the life: he that believeth in me, though he were dead, yet shall he live: 26And whosoever liveth and believeth in me shall never die. Believest thou this?

Acts 1:3

To whom also he shewed himself alive after his passion by many infallible proofs, being seen of them forty days, and speaking of the things pertaining to the kingdom of God:

Acts 2:24

Whom God hath raised up, having loosed the pains of death: because it was not possible that he should be holden of it.

Acts 2:32

This Jesus hath God raised up, whereof we all are witnesses.

Acts 3:15

And killed the Prince of life, whom God hath raised from the dead; whereof we are witnesses.

Acts 3:26

Unto you first God, having raised up his Son Jesus, sent him to bless you, in turning away every one of you from his iniquities.

Acts 4:10

Be it known unto you all, and to all the people of Israel, that by the name of Jesus Christ of Nazareth, whom ye crucified, whom God raised from the dead, even by him doth this man stand here before you whole.

Acts 9: 4,5

And he fell to the earth, and heard a voice saying unto him, Saul, Saul, why persecutest thou me?

And he said, Who art thou, Lord? And the Lord said, I am Jesus whom thou persecutest: it is hard for thee to kick against the pricks.

Acts 13: 30-38

But God raised him from the dead:

And he was seen many days of them which came up with him from Galilee to Jerusalem, who are his witnesses unto the people.

And we declare unto you glad tidings, how that the promise which was made unto the fathers,

God hath fulfilled the same unto us their children, in that he hath raised up Jesus again; as it is also written in the second psalm, Thou art my Son, this day have I begotten thee.

And as concerning that he raised him up from the dead, now no more to return to corruption, he said on this wise, I will give you the sure mercies of David.

Wherefore he saith also in another psalm, Thou shalt not suffer thine Holy One to see corruption.

For David, after he had served his own generation by the will of God, fell on sleep, and was laid unto his fathers, and saw corruption:

But he, whom God raised again, saw no corruption.

Be it known unto you therefore, men and brethren, that through this man is preached unto you the forgiveness of sins:

Acts 26:18

To open their eyes, and to turn them from darkness to light, and from the power of Satan unto God, that they may receive forgiveness of sins, and inheritance among them which are sanctified by faith that is in me.

Acts 17:30,31

And the times of this ignorance God winked at; but now commandeth all men every where to repent:

Because he hath appointed a day, in the which he will judge the world in righteousness by that man whom he hath ordained; whereof he hath given assurance unto all men, in that he hath raised him from the dead.

Romans 1:1-4

Paul, a servant of Jesus Christ, called to be an apostle, separated unto the gospel of God,

(Which he had promised afore by his prophets in the holy scriptures,)

Concerning his Son Jesus Christ our Lord, which was made of the seed of David according to the flesh;

And declared to be the Son of God with power, according to the spirit of holiness, by the resurrection from the dead:

Romans 5:10

For if, when we were enemies, we were reconciled to God by the death of his Son, much more, being reconciled, we shall be saved by his life.

Romans 6:4,5

Therefore we are buried with him by baptism into death: that like as Christ was raised up from the dead by the glory of the Father, even so we also should walk in newness of life.

For if we have been planted together in the likeness of his death, we shall be also in the likeness of his resurrection:

Romans 6:23

For the wages of sin is death; but the gift of God is eternal life through Jesus Christ our Lord.

Romans 10:9

That if thou shalt confess with thy mouth the Lord Jesus, and shalt believe in thine heart that God hath raised him from the dead, thou shalt be saved.

1 Corinthians 6:14

And God hath both raised up the Lord, and will also raise up us by his own power.

1 Corinthians 15:1-8

Moreover, brethren, I declare unto you the gospel which I preached unto you, which also ye have received, and wherein ye stand;

By which also ye are saved, if ye keep in memory what I preached unto you, unless ye have believed in vain.

For I delivered unto you first of all that which I also received, how that Christ died for our sins according to the scriptures;

And that he was buried, and that he rose again the third day according to the scriptures:

And that he was seen of Cephas, then of the twelve:

After that, he was seen of above five hundred brethren at once; of whom the greater part remain unto this present, but some are fallen asleep.

After that, he was seen of James; then of all the apostles.

And last of all he was seen of me also, as of one born out of due time.

1 Corinthians 15:20

But now is Christ risen from the dead, and become the firstfruits of them that slept.

2 Corinthians 4:14

Knowing that he which raised up the Lord Jesus shall raise up us also by Jesus, and shall present us with you.

Ephesians 1:20

Which he wrought in Christ, when he raised him from the dead, and set him at his own right hand in the heavenly places,

Colossians 3: 1-3

If ye then be risen with Christ, seek those things which are above, where Christ sitteth on the right hand of God.

Set your affection on things above, not on things on the earth.

For ye are dead, and your life is hid with Christ in God.

Colossians 2:12

Buried with him in baptism, wherein also ye are risen with him through the faith of the operation of God, who hath raised him from the dead.

1 Thessalonians 1:10

And to wait for his Son from heaven, whom he raised from the dead, even Jesus, which delivered us from the wrath to come.

1 Timothy 3:16

And without controversy great is the mystery of godliness: God was manifest in the flesh, justified in the Spirit, seen of angels, preached unto the Gentiles, believed on in the world, received up into glory.

Hebrews 13:20

Now the God of peace, that brought again from the dead our Lord Jesus, that great shepherd of the sheep, through the blood of the everlasting covenant,

1 Peter 1 :18-20

Forasmuch as ye know that ye were not redeemed with corruptible things, as silver and gold, from your vain conversation received by tradition from your fathers;

But with the precious blood of Christ, as of a lamb without blemish and without spot:

Who verily was foreordained before the foundation of the world, but was manifest in these last times for you,

1 John 5:13

These things have I written unto you that believe on the name of the Son of God; that ye may know that ye have eternal life, and that ye may believe on the name of the Son of God.

THE ASCENSION OF OUR LORD JESUS CHRIST

Following His resurrection from the dead, Jesus appeared among His disciples during a period of forty days to complete His teaching among them and to bring them utter assurance of His conquest of death and the coming of God's Kingdom, through Him.

The apostles saw the LORD gathered up into a cloud and disappear from view.

Matthew 28: 5,6

> *And the angel answered and said unto the women, Fear not ye: for I know that ye seek Jesus, which was crucified.*
>
> *He is not here: for he is risen, as he said. Come, see the place where the Lord lay.*

Matthew 28:16

> *Then the eleven disciples went away into Galilee, into a mountain where Jesus had appointed them.*

Luke 24:50-53

> *And he led them out as far as to Bethany, and he lifted up his hands, and blessed them.*

And it came to pass, while he blessed them, he was parted from them, and carried up into heaven.

And they worshipped him, and returned to Jerusalem with great joy:

And were continually in the temple, praising and blessing God. Amen.

Acts 1: 1-11

.. of all that Jesus began both to do and teach, until the day in which He was taken up, after that He, through the Holy Ghost, had given commandments unto the apostles whom He had chosen: To whom also He showed Himself alive after His passion by many infallible proofs, being seen of them forty days, and speaking the things pertaining to the Kingdom of God.

And being assembled together with them, commanded them that they should not depart from Jerusalem, but wait for the promise of the Father, which, says He, ye have heard of Me.

For John truly baptized with water; but ye shall be baptized with the Holy Ghost not many days hence.

When they therefore were come together, they asked of Him, saying, LORD, wilt thou at this time restore again the Kingdom to Israel? And He said unto them, It is not for you to know the times or the seasons which the Father has put in His own power.

But ye shall receive power, after that the Holy Ghost is come upon you: and ye shall be witnesses unto Me both in Jerusalem, and in all Judæa, and in Samaria, and unto the uttermost part of the earth.

And when He had spoken these things, while they beheld, He was taken up and a cloud received Him out of their sight.

OUR LORD JESUS CHRIST IS SAVIOR OF THE WORLD

Matthew 1:21

And she shall bring forth a son, and thou shalt call his name JESUS: for he shall save his people from their sins.

Mark 16:16

He that believeth and is baptized shall be saved; but he that believeth not shall be damned.

Luke 2:11

For unto you is born this day in the city of David a Saviour, which is Christ the Lord.

John 1:29

The next day John seeth Jesus coming unto him, and saith, Behold the Lamb of God, which taketh away the sin of the world.

John 3:14-18

And as Moses lifted up the serpent in the wilderness, even so must the Son of man be lifted up:

That whosoever believeth in him should not perish, but have eternal life.

For God so loved the world, that he gave his only begotten Son, that whosoever believeth in him should not perish, but have everlasting life.

For God sent not his Son into the world to condemn the world; but that the world through him might be saved.

He that believeth on him is not condemned: but he that believeth not is condemned already, because he hath not believed in the name of the only begotten Son of God.

John 3:35,36
The Father loveth the Son, and hath given all things into his hand.

He that believeth on the Son hath everlasting life: and he that believeth not the Son shall not see life; but the wrath of God abideth on him.

John 6:32,33
Then Jesus said unto them, Verily, verily, I say unto you, Moses gave you not that bread from heaven; but my Father giveth you the true bread from heaven.

For the bread of God is he which cometh down from heaven, and giveth life unto the world.

John 6:47-51
Verily, verily, I say unto you, He that believeth on me hath everlasting life. I am that bread of life. Your

fathers did eat manna in the wilderness, and are dead. This is the bread which cometh down from heaven, that a man may eat thereof, and not die. I am the living bread which came down from heaven: if any man eat of this bread, he shall live for ever: and the bread that I will give is my flesh, which I will give for the life of the world.

John 8:23,24

And he said unto them, Ye are from beneath; I am from above: ye are of this world; I am not of this world.

I said therefore unto you, that ye shall die in your sins: for if ye believe not that I am he, ye shall die in your sins.

John 8:51

Verily, verily, I say unto you, If a man keep my saying, he shall never see death.

John 10:15

As the Father knoweth me, even so know I the Father: and I lay down my life for the sheep.

John 10:27

My sheep hear my voice, and I know them, and they follow me:

John 12:48

He that rejecteth me, and receiveth not my words, hath one that judgeth him: the word that I have spoken, the same shall judge him in the last day.

John 14:16

And I will pray the Father, and he shall give you another Comforter, that he may abide with you for ever;

Acts 2:21

And it shall come to pass, that whosoever shall call on the name of the Lord shall be saved.

Romans 10:13

For whosoever shall call upon the name of the Lord shall be saved.

Acts 3:19-23

Repent ye therefore, and be converted, that your sins may be blotted out, when the times of refreshing shall come from the presence of the Lord.

And he shall send Jesus Christ, which before was preached unto you:

Whom the heaven must receive until the times of restitution of all things, which God hath spoken by the mouth of all his holy prophets since the world began.

For Moses truly said unto the fathers, A prophet shall the Lord your God raise up unto you of your brethren, like unto me; him shall ye hear in all things whatsoever he shall say unto you.

And it shall come to pass, that every soul, which will not hear that prophet, shall be destroyed from among the people.

Acts 3:26

> *Unto you first God, having raised up his Son Jesus, sent him to bless you, in turning away every one of you from his iniquities.*

Acts 4:12

> *Neither is there salvation in any other: for there is none other name under heaven given among men, whereby we must be saved.*

Acts 5:31

> *Him hath God exalted with his right hand to be a Prince and a Saviour, for to give repentance to Israel, and forgiveness of sins.*

Acts 16:30

> *And brought them out, and said, Sirs, what must I do to be saved?*

Romans 3:23,24

> *For all have sinned, and come short of the glory of God; Being justified freely by his grace through the redemption that is in Christ Jesus:*

Romans 5:8,9

> *But God commendeth his love toward us, in that, while we were yet sinners, Christ died for us.*

> *Much more then, being now justified by his blood, we shall be saved from wrath through him.*

Romans 10:9

> That if thou shalt confess with thy mouth the Lord Jesus, and shalt believe in thine heart that God hath raised him from the dead, thou shalt be saved. For whosoever shall call upon the name of the Lord shall be saved.

2 Corinthians 6:22

> (For he saith, I have heard thee in a time accepted, and in the day of salvation have I succoured thee: behold, now is the accepted time; behold, now is the day of salvation.)

Galatians 1:3,4

> Grace be to you and peace from God the Father, and from our Lord Jesus Christ,

> Who gave himself for our sins, that he might deliver us from this present evil world, according to the will of God and our Father:

Ephesians 2:8.9

> For by grace are ye saved through faith; and that not of yourselves: it is the gift of God:

> Not of works, lest any man should boast.

1 Timothy 1:15

> This is a faithful saying, and worthy of all acceptation, that Christ Jesus came into the world to save sinners; of whom I am chief.

1 Timothy 4:10

For therefore we both labour and suffer reproach, because we trust in the living God, who is the Saviour of all men, specially of those that believe.

2 Timothy 3:15-17

And that from a child thou hast known the holy scriptures, which are able to make thee wise unto salvation through faith which is in Christ Jesus.

All scripture is given by inspiration of God, and is profitable for doctrine, for reproof, for correction, for instruction in righteousness:

That the man of God may be perfect, thoroughly furnished unto all good works.

Titus 3:4

But after that the kindness and love of God our Saviour toward man appeared,

Not by works of righteousness which we have done, but according to his mercy he saved us, by the washing of regeneration, and renewing of the Holy Ghost;

1 Peter 1:18-20

Forasmuch as ye know that ye were not redeemed with corruptible things, as silver and gold, from your vain conversation received by tradition from your fathers;

But with the precious blood of Christ, as of a lamb without blemish and without spot:

Who verily was foreordained before the foundation of the world, but was manifest in these last times for you,

1 John 4:19

We love him, because he first loved us.

1 John 4:14,15

And we have seen and do testify that the Father sent the Son to be the Saviour of the world.

Whosoever shall confess that Jesus is the Son of God, God dwelleth in him, and he in God.

1 John 5:11,12

And this is the record, that God hath given to us eternal life, and this life is in his Son.

He that hath the Son hath life; and he that hath not the Son of God hath not life.

Revelation 3:20

Behold, I stand at the door, and knock: if any man hear my voice, and open the door, I will come in to him, and will sup with him, and he with me.

Zechariah 9:9

Rejoice greatly, O daughter of Zion; shout, O daughter of Jerusalem: behold, thy King cometh unto thee: he is just, and having salvation; lowly, and riding upon an ass, and upon a colt the foal of an ass.

LORD JESUS CHRIST – OUR SIN BEARER

John 1:29

> The next day John seeth Jesus coming unto him, and saith, Behold the Lamb of God, which taketh away the sin of the world.

Romans 4:25

> Who was delivered for our offences, and was raised again for our justification.

1 Corinthians 15:3

> For I delivered unto you first of all that which I also received, how that Christ died for our sins according to the scriptures;

2 Corinthians 5:21

> For he hath made him to be sin for us, who knew no sin; that we might be made the righteousness of God in him.

1 Peter 2:24

> Who his own self bare our sins in his own body on the tree, that we, being dead to sins, should live unto righteousness: by whose stripes ye were healed.

Hebrews 9:27
> *And as it is appointed unto men once to die, but after this the judgment:*

1 John 3:5
> *And ye know that he was manifested to take away our sins; and in him is no sin.*

LORD JESUS CHRIST – FORGIVER OF SINS

Matthew 9:6
But that ye may know that the Son of man hath power on earth to forgive sins, (then saith he to the sick of the palsy,) Arise, take up thy bed, and go unto thine house.

Matthew 26:28
For this is my blood of the new testament, which is shed for many for the remission of sins.

Mark 2:5
When Jesus saw their faith, he said unto the sick of the palsy, Son, thy sins be forgiven thee.

Mark 2:10
But that ye may know that the Son of man hath power on earth to forgive sins, (he saith to the sick of the palsy,)

Luke 5:24
But that ye may know that the Son of man hath power upon earth to forgive sins, (he said unto the sick of the

palsy,) I say unto thee, Arise, and take up thy couch, and go into thine house.

Luke 7:47

Wherefore I say unto thee, Her sins, which are many, are forgiven; for she loved much: but to whom little is forgiven, the same loveth little.

Acts 2:38

Then Peter said unto them, Repent, and be baptized every one of you in the name of Jesus Christ for the remission of sins, and ye shall receive the gift of the Holy Ghost.

Acts 5:31

Him hath God exalted with his right hand to be a Prince and a Saviour, for to give repentance to Israel, and forgiveness of sins.

Acts 10:42,43

To him give all the prophets witness, that through his name whosoever believeth in him shall receive remission of sins.

Acts 13:38

Be it known unto you therefore, men and brethren, that through this man is preached unto you the forgiveness of sins:

Ephesians 1:7

In whom we have redemption through his blood, the forgiveness of sins, according to the riches of his grace;

Colossians 1:13,14

> *Who hath delivered us from the power of darkness, and hath translated us into the kingdom of his dear Son: In whom we have redemption through his blood, even the forgiveness of sins:*

1 John 1:9

> *If we confess our sins, he is faithful and just to forgive us our sins, and to cleanse us from all unrighteousness.*

LORD JESUS CHRIST RECEIVED HONOUR AND WORSHIP

Matthew 2: 2

Saying, Where is he that is born King of the Jews? for we have seen his star in the east, and are come to worship him.

Matthew 14: 33

Then they that were in the ship came and worshipped him, saying, Of a truth thou art the Son of God.

Matthew 15: 25

Then came she and worshipped him, saying, Lord, help me.

Matthew 28: 7-9

And go quickly, and tell his disciples that he is risen from the dead; and, behold, he goeth before you into Galilee; there shall ye see him: lo, I have told you.

And they departed quickly from the sepulchre with fear and great joy; and did run to bring his disciples word.

And as they went to tell his disciples, behold, Jesus met them, saying, All hail. And they came and held him by the feet, and worshipped him.

Matthew 28: 16,17

Then the eleven disciples went away into Galilee, into a mountain where Jesus had appointed them.

And when they saw him, they worshipped him: but some doubted.

Luke 24: 51,52

And it came to pass, while he blessed them, he was parted from them, and carried up into heaven.

And they worshipped him, and returned to Jerusalem with great joy:

John 5: 23

That all men should honour the Son, even as they honour the Father. He that honoureth not the Son honoureth not the Father which hath sent him.

Hebrews 1: 6

And again, when he bringeth in the firstbegotten into the world, he saith, And let all the angels of God worship him.

Revelation 5: 6-14

And I beheld, and, lo, in the midst of the throne and of the four beasts, and in the midst of the elders, stood a Lamb as it had been slain, having seven horns and seven eyes, which are the seven Spirits of God sent forth into all the earth.

And he came and took the book out of the right hand of him that sat upon the throne.

And when he had taken the book, the four beasts and four and twenty elders fell down before the Lamb, having every one of them harps, and golden vials full of odours, which are the prayers of saints.

And they sung a new song, saying, Thou art worthy to take the book, and to open the seals thereof: for thou wast slain, and hast redeemed us to God by thy blood out of every kindred, and tongue, and people, and nation;

And hast made us unto our God kings and priests: and we shall reign on the earth.

And I beheld, and I heard the voice of many angels round about the throne and the beasts and the elders: and the number of them was ten thousand times ten thousand, and thousands of thousands;

Saying with a loud voice, Worthy is the Lamb that was slain to receive power, and riches, and wisdom, and strength, and honour, and glory, and blessing.

And every creature which is in heaven, and on the earth, and under the earth, and such as are in the sea, and all that are in them, heard I saying, Blessing, and honour, and glory, and power, be unto him that sitteth upon the throne, and unto the Lamb for ever and ever.

And the four beasts said, Amen. And the four and twenty elders fell down and worshipped him that liveth for ever and ever.

LORD JESUS CHRIST IS JUDGE OF THE LIVING AND THE DEAD

Matthew 25:31,32

When the Son of man shall come in his glory, and all the holy angels with him, then shall he sit upon the throne of his glory:

And before him shall be gathered all nations: and he shall separate them one from another, as a shepherd divideth his sheep from the goats:

John 5:22-26

For the Father judgeth no man, but hath committed all judgment unto the Son:

That all men should honour the Son, even as they honour the Father. He that honoureth not the Son honoureth not the Father which hath sent him.

Verily, verily, I say unto you, He that heareth my word, and believeth on him that sent me, hath everlasting life, and shall not come into condemnation; but is passed from death unto life.

Verily, verily, I say unto you, The hour is coming, and now is, when the dead shall hear the voice of the Son of God: and they that hear shall live.

For as the Father hath life in himself; so hath he given to the Son to have life in himself;

John 12:48

He that rejecteth me, and receiveth not my words, hath one that judgeth him: the word that I have spoken, the same shall judge him in the last day.

Acts 10:42

And he commanded us to preach unto the people, and to testify that it is he which was ordained of God to be the Judge of quick and dead.

Acts 17:30.31

And the times of this ignorance God winked at; but now commandeth all men every where to repent:

Because he hath appointed a day, in the which he will judge the world in righteousness by that man whom he hath ordained; whereof he hath given assurance unto all men, in that he hath raised him from the dead.

Romans 2:16

In the day when God shall judge the secrets of men by Jesus Christ according to my gospel.

Romans 14:10

But why dost thou judge thy brother? or why dost thou set at nought thy brother? for we shall all stand before the judgment seat of Christ.

2 Corinthians 5:10

For we must all appear before the judgment seat of Christ; that every one may receive the things done in his body, according to that he hath done, whether it be good or bad.

Hebrews 9:27

And as it is appointed unto men once to die, but after this the judgment:

Revelation 20:11-15

And I saw a great white throne, and him that sat on it, from whose face the earth and the heaven fled away; and there was found no place for them.

And I saw the dead, small and great, stand before God; and the books were opened: and another book was opened, which is the book of life: and the dead were judged out of those things which were written in the books, according to their works.

And the sea gave up the dead which were in it; and death and hell delivered up the dead which were in them: and they were judged every man according to their works. And death and hell were cast into the lake of fire. This is the second death.

And whosoever was not found written in the book of life was cast into the lake of fire.

LORD JESUS CHRIST'S VICTORY OVER SIN AND DEATH

Matthew 28:18-20

And Jesus came and spake unto them, saying, All power is given unto me in heaven and in earth.

Go ye therefore, and teach all nations, baptizing them in the name of the Father, and of the Son, and of the Holy Ghost:

Teaching them to observe all things whatsoever I have commanded you: and, lo, I am with you always, even unto the end of the world. Amen.

Luke 10:19

Behold, I give unto you power to tread on serpents and scorpions, and over all the power of the enemy: and nothing shall by any means hurt you.

John 16:33

These things I have spoken unto you, that in me ye might have peace. In the world ye shall have tribulation: but be of good cheer; I have overcome the world.

1 Corinthians 15:57

But thanks be to God, which giveth us the victory through our Lord Jesus Christ.

Colossians 2:15

And having spoiled principalities and powers, he made a shew of them openly, triumphing over them in it.

2 Thessalonians 2:8

And then shall that Wicked be revealed, whom the Lord shall consume with the spirit of his mouth, and shall destroy with the brightness of his coming:

Hebrews 2:14

Forasmuch then as the children are partakers of flesh and blood, he also   himself likewise took part of the same; that through death he might destroy him that had the power of death, that is, the devil;

Hebrews 5:9

And being made perfect, he became the author of eternal salvation unto all them that obey him;

1 John 3:8

He that committeth sin is of the devil; for the devil sinneth from the beginning. For this purpose the Son of God was manifested, that he might destroy the works of the devil.

Revelation 12:11

And they overcame him by the blood of the Lamb, and by the word of their testimony; and they loved not their lives unto the death.

Revelation 19:11-16

And I saw heaven opened, and behold a white horse; and he that sat upon him was called Faithful and True, and in righteousness he doth judge and make war.

His eyes were as a flame of fire, and on his head were many crowns; and he had a name written, that no man knew, but he himself.

And he was clothed with a vesture dipped in blood: and his name is called The Word of God.

And the armies which were in heaven followed him upon white horses, clothed in fine linen, white and clean.

And out of his mouth goeth a sharp sword, that with it he should smite the nations: and he shall rule them with a rod of iron: and he treadeth the winepress of the fierceness and wrath of Almighty God.

And he hath on his vesture and on his thigh a name written, KING OF KINGS, AND LORD OF LORDS.

LORD JESUS CHRIST – SIGNS OF HIS SECOND COMING

WARNING SIGNS WILL HERALD HIS RETURN :-

Luke 21:28

> And when these things begin to come to pass, then look up, and lift up your heads; for your redemption draweth nigh.

FALSE CHRISTS AND RUMOURS OF WAR

Matthew 24:4-6

> And Jesus answered and said unto them, Take heed that no man deceive you.

> For many shall come in my name, saying, I am Christ; and shall deceive many.

> And ye shall hear of wars and rumours of wars: see that ye be not troubled: for all these things must come to pass, but the end is not yet.

FAMINE AND PESTILENCE, EARTHQUAKES

Matthew 24:7

For nation shall rise against nation, and kingdom against kingdom: and there shall be famines, and pestilences, and earthquakes, in divers places.

INCREASED HATRED AND ALIENATION

Jesus warned of a worldwide hatred of the Jews that would signal His impending return.

Matthew 24:9

Then shall they deliver you up to be afflicted, and shall kill you: and ye shall be hated of all nations for my name's sake.

Matthew 24:10-12

And then shall many be offended, and shall betray one another, and shall hate one another. And many false prophets shall rise, and shall deceive many. And because iniquity shall abound, the love of many shall wax cold.

Contents of this page taken from:
KJV Prophecy Study Bible – General Editor, Grant R. Jeffrey
Article 'Signs of the Second Coming' on pages 1108-1110

WORLDWIDE EVANGELISM

Matthew 24:14

And this gospel of the kingdom shall be preached in all the world for a witness unto all nations; and then shall the end come.

STAY ALERT

The church is called to vigilance against all that would deny the truth of God, and in particular the full deity and true humanity of His eternal Son.

We are not to be idle, but rather by life and witness confront the powers of antichrist at large in the world in our generation.

The really important factor is our moral attitudes: what we are, our desire to do the Lord's will, and to encourage others to a similar obedience. The correct attitude is one of watchfulness, recognising that the conflict between good and evil will sharpen before the end.

1 Thessalonians 4:16,17

For the Lord himself shall descend from heaven with a shout, with the voice of the archangel, and with the trump of God: and the dead in Christ shall rise first:

Then we who are alive and remain shall be caught up together with them in the clouds, to meet the Lord in the air: and so shall we ever be with the Lord.

Contents of this page taken from:
KJV Prophecy Study Bible – General Editor, Grant R. Jeffrey
Article 'Signs of the Second Coming' on pages 1108-1110

LORD JESUS CHRIST – SINLESS SON OF GOD

Hebrews 4:15 (Jesus speaking)

… was in all points tempted like as we are, yet without sin.

1 Peter 2:22

… who did no sin, neither was guile found in His mouth

2 Corinthians 5:21

For He has made Him to be sin for us, who knew no sin; …

THE BELIEVER'S AUTHORITY
IN CHRIST JESUS

Matthew 10:1

*And when he had called unto him his twelve disciples,
he gave them authority against unclean spirits, to cast
them out, and to heal all manner of sickness and all
manner of disease.*

Matthew 10;7,8

*And as ye go, preach, saying, The kingdom of heaven is
at hand. Heal the sick, cleanse the lepers, raise the dead,
cast out devils: freely ye have received, freely give.*

Matthew 28:18-20

*And Jesus came and spake unto them, saying, All power
is given unto me in heaven and in earth.*

*Go ye therefore, and teach all nations, baptizing them
in the name of the Father, and of the Son, and of the
Holy Ghost:*

*Teaching them to observe all things whatsoever I have
commanded you: and, lo, I am with you always, even
unto the end of the world. Amen.*

Mark 11:23-26

*For verily I say unto you, That whosoever shall say
unto this mountain, Be thou removed, and be thou
cast into the sea; and shall not doubt in his heart, but
shall believe that those things which he saith shall come
to pass; he shall have whatsoever he saith.*

Therefore I say unto you, What things soever ye desire, when ye pray, believe that ye receive them, and ye shall have them.

And when ye stand praying, forgive, if ye have ought against any: that your Father also which is in heaven may forgive you your trespasses.

But if ye do not forgive, neither will your Father which is in heaven forgive your trespasses.

Mark 16:15-18

And he said unto them, Go ye into all the world, and preach the gospel to every creature. He that believeth and is baptized shall be saved; but he that believeth not shall be damned. And these signs shall follow them that believe; in my name shall they cast out devils; they shall speak with new tongues; They shall take up serpents; and if they drink any deadly thing, it shall not hurt them; they shall lay hands on the sick, and they shall recover.

Luke 10:19

Behold, I give unto you power to tread on serpents and scorpions, and over all the power of the enemy: and nothing shall by any means hurt you.

John 14:20

At that day ye shall know that I am in my Father, and ye in me, and I in you.

Romans 5:17

For if by one man's offence death reigned by one; much more they which receive abundance of grace and of the gift of righteousness shall reign in life by one, Jesus Christ.)

1 Corinthians 6:19

What? know ye not that your body is the temple of the Holy Ghost which is in you, which ye have of God, and ye are not your own?

Ephesians 1:1

Paul, an apostle of Jesus Christ by the will of God, to the saints which are at Ephesus, and to the faithful in Christ Jesus:

Ephesians 1:4

According as he hath chosen us in him before the foundation of the world, that we should be holy and without blame before him in love:

Ephesians 1:13

In whom ye also trusted, after that ye heard the word of truth, the gospel of your salvation: in whom also after that ye believed, ye were sealed with that Holy Spirit of promise,

Ephesians 2:6

And hath raised us up together, and made us sit together in heavenly places in Christ Jesus:

Ephesians 4:6

One God and Father of all, who is above all, and through all, and in you all.

Colossians 1:13-22

Who hath delivered us from the power of darkness, and hath translated us into the kingdom of his dear Son:

In whom we have redemption through his blood, even the forgiveness of sins:

Who is the image of the invisible God, the firstborn of every creature:

For by him were all things created, that are in heaven, and that are in earth, visible and invisible, whether they be thrones, or dominions, or principalities, or powers: all things were created by him, and for him:

And he is before all things, and by him all things consist.

And he is the head of the body, the church: who is the beginning, the firstborn from the dead; that in all things he might have the preeminence.

For it pleased the Father that in him should all fullness dwell;

And, having made peace through the blood of his cross, by him to reconcile all things unto himself; by him, I say, whether they be things in earth, or things in heaven.

And you, that were sometime alienated and enemies in your mind by wicked works, yet now hath he reconciled

In the body of his flesh through death, to present you holy and unblameable and unreproveable in his sight:

Colossians 2:15

And having spoiled principalities and powers, he made a show of them openly, triumphing over them in it.

Colossians 3:1-4

If ye then be risen with Christ, seek those things which are above, where Christ sitteth on the right hand of God.

Set your affection on things above, not on things on the earth.

For ye are dead, and your life is hid with Christ in God.

When Christ, who is our life, shall appear, then shall ye also appear with him in glory.

Hebrews 2:14

Forasmuch then as the children are partakers of flesh and blood, he also himself likewise took part of the same; that through death he might destroy him that had the power of death, that is, the devil;

1 John 3:8

He that committeth sin is of the devil; for the devil sinneth from the beginning. For this purpose the Son of God was manifested, that he might destroy the works of the devil.

Revelation 12:11

And they overcame him by the blood of the Lamb, and by the word of their testimony; and they loved not their lives unto the death.

WHO BELIEVERS ARE
IN CHRIST

WE ARE CHILDREN, SONS AND HEIRS OF GOD

Romans 8:16,17

The Spirit itself beareth witness with our spirit, that we are the children of God: And if children, then heirs; heirs of God, and joint-heirs with Christ; if so be that we suffer with him, that we may be also glorified together.

John 1:12

But as many as received him, to them gave he power to become the sons of God, even to them that believe on his name:

Galatians 4:6,7

And because ye are sons, God hath sent forth the Spirit of his Son into your hearts, crying, Abba, Father. Therefore thou art no more a servant, but a son; and if a son, then an heir of God through Christ.

WE HAVE MORE THAN ABUNDANT LIFE

John 10:10

The thief cometh not, but for to steal, and to kill, and to destroy: I am come that they might have life, and that they might have it more abundantly.

Psalm 36:7

> How excellent is thy loving-kindness, O God! therefore the children of men put their trust under the shadow of thy wings.

> They shall be abundantly satisfied with the fatness of thy house; and thou shalt make them drink of the river of thy pleasures.

WE ARE WITNESSES FOR CHRIST

Acts 1:8

> But ye shall receive power, after that the Holy Ghost is come upon you: and ye shall be witnesses unto me both in Jerusalem, and in all Judaea, and in Samaria, and unto the uttermost part of the earth.

WE ARE MORE THAN CONQUERORS

Romans 8:37

> In all these things we are more than conquerors through him that loved us.

OUR MINDS ARE RENEWED

Romans 12:2

> And be not conformed to this world: but be ye transformed by the renewing of your mind, that ye may prove what is that good, and acceptable, and perfect, will of God.

WE HAVE THE MIND OF CHRIST

1 Corinthians 2:16

> *For who hath known the mind of the Lord, that he may instruct him? but we have the mind of Christ.*

WE ARE PROSPEROUS IN ALL AREAS OF OUR LIVES

Deuteronomy 7:13-16

> *And he will love thee, and bless thee, and multiply thee: he will also bless the fruit of thy womb, and the fruit of thy land, thy corn, and thy wine, and thine oil, the increase of thy kine, and the flocks of thy sheep, in the land which he sware unto thy fathers to give thee.*
>
> *Thou shalt be blessed above all people: there shall not be male or female barren among you, or among your cattle.*
>
> *And the LORD will take away from thee all sickness, and will put none of the evil diseases of Egypt, which thou knowest, upon thee; but will lay them upon all them that hate thee.*
>
> *And thou shalt consume all the people which the LORD thy God shall deliver thee; thine eye shall have no pity upon them: neither shalt thou serve their gods; for that will be a snare unto thee.*

Deuteronomy 8:18

> *But thou shalt remember the LORD thy God: for it is he that giveth thee power to get wealth, that he may*

establish his covenant which he sware unto thy fathers, as it is this day.

Psalms 84:11

For the LORD God is a sun and shield: the LORD will give grace and glory: no good thing will he withhold from them that walk uprightly.

Psalms 112:3

Praise ye the LORD. Blessed is the man that feareth the LORD, that delighteth greatly in his commandments. His seed shall be mighty upon earth: the generation of the upright shall be blessed. Wealth and riches shall be in his house: and his righteousness endureth for ever.

Proverbs 10:22

The blessing of the LORD, it maketh rich, and he addeth no sorrow with it.

2 Corinthians 9:8

And God is able to make all grace abound toward you; that ye, always having all sufficiency in all things, may abound to every good work:

1 Timothy 6:17

The LORD gives us richly all things to enjoy.

WE ARE CRUCIFIED WITH CHRIST

Galatians 2:20
> *I am crucified with Christ: nevertheless I live; yet not I, but Christ liveth in me: and the life which I now live in the flesh I live by the faith of the Son of God, who loved me, and gave himself for me.*

WE ARE MADE RIGHTEOUS

Philippians 3:9
> *And be found in him, not having mine own righteousness, which is of the law, but that which is through the faith of Christ, the righteousness which is of God by faith:*

WE ARE STRENGTHENED

Philippians 4:13
> *I can do all things through Christ which strengtheneth me.*

WE ARE RISEN WITH CHRIST AND OUR LIFE IS HIDDEN WITH CHRIST IN GOD

Colossians 3:1-4
> *If ye then be risen with Christ, seek those things which are above, where Christ sitteth on the right hand of God.*

Set your affection on things above, not on things on the earth. For ye are dead, and your life is hid with Christ in God.

When Christ, who is our life, shall appear, then shall ye also appear with him in glory.

WE ARE THE ELECT

1 Peter 1:2
Elect according to the foreknowledge of God the Father, through sanctification of the Spirit, unto obedience and sprinkling of the blood of Jesus Christ: Grace unto you, and peace, be multiplied.

WE ARE A ROYAL PRIESTHOOD AND A HOLY NATION AND CHOSEN OF GOD

1 Peter 2:9
But ye are a chosen generation, a royal priesthood, an holy nation, a peculiar people; that ye should shew forth the praises of him who hath called you out of darkness into his marvellous light.

WE ARE PARTAKERS OF THE DIVINE NATURE

2 Peter 1:4
Whereby are given unto us exceeding great and precious promises: that by these ye might be partakers of the

divine nature, having escaped the corruption that is in the world through lust.

WE ARE BEING CLEANSED

1 John 1:9

If we confess our sins, he is faithful and just to forgive us our sins, and to cleanse us from all unrighteousness.

WE ARE OVERCOMERS

1 John 4:4

Ye are of God, little children, and have overcome them: because greater is he that is in you, than he that is in the world.

WE ARE COMPLETELY BLESSED

Deuteronomy 28:1-14

And it shall come to pass, if thou shalt hearken diligently unto the voice of the LORD thy God, to observe and to do all his commandments which I command thee this day, that the LORD thy God will set thee on high above all nations of the earth:

And all these blessings shall come on thee, and overtake thee, if thou shalt hearken unto the voice of the LORD thy God.

Blessed shalt thou be in the city, and blessed shalt thou be in the field.

Blessed shall be the fruit of thy body, and the fruit of thy ground, and the fruit of thy cattle, the increase of thy kine, and the flocks of thy sheep.

Blessed shall be thy basket and thy store.

Blessed shalt thou be when thou comest in, and blessed shalt thou be when thou goest out.

The LORD shall cause thine enemies that rise up against thee to be smitten before thy face: they shall come out against thee one way, and flee before thee seven ways.

The LORD shall command the blessing upon thee in thy storehouses, and in all that thou settest thine hand unto; and he shall bless thee in the land which the LORD thy God giveth thee.

The LORD shall establish thee an holy people unto himself, as he hath sworn unto thee, if thou shalt keep the commandments of the LORD thy God, and walk in his ways.

And all people of the earth shall see that thou art called by the name of the LORD; and they shall be afraid of thee.

And the LORD shall make thee plenteous in goods, in the fruit of thy body, and in the fruit of thy cattle, and in the fruit of thy ground, in the land which the LORD sware unto thy fathers to give thee.

The LORD shall open unto thee his good treasure, the heaven to give the rain unto thy land in his season, and to bless all the work of thine hand: and thou shalt lend unto many nations, and thou shalt not borrow.

And the LORD shall make thee the head, and not the tail; and thou shalt be above only, and thou shalt not be beneath; if that thou hearken unto the commandments of the LORD thy God, which I command thee this day, to observe and to do them:

And thou shalt not go aside from any of the words which I command thee this day, to the right hand, or to the left, to go after other gods to serve them.

Ephesians 1:1

We are blessed with every spiritual blessing in heavenly places in Christ.

SALVATION SCRIPTURES

THE ROAD TO SALVATION

We Are All Sinners

Romans 3:23
> *For all have sinned and fall short of the glory of God*

God Almighty Is Without Sin

Psalm 18:30
> *As for God, his way is perfect: the word of the LORD is tried: he is a buckler to all those that trust in him.*

God Cannot Look Upon Sin

Isaiah 59:2
> *But your iniquities have separated between you and your God, and your sins have hid his face from you, that he will not hear.*

What Is God's Punishment For Sin?

Romans 6:23
> *For the wages of sin is death; but the gift of God is eternal life through Jesus Christ our Lord.*

WE HAVE ALL INHERITED THE SINFUL NATURE FROM ADAM

Exodus 20:5

> *Thou shalt not bow down thyself to them, nor serve them: for I the LORD thy God am a jealous God, visiting the iniquity of the fathers upon the children unto the third and fourth generation of them that hate me;*

Deuteronomy 5:9

> *Thou shalt not bow down thyself unto them, nor serve them: for I the LORD thy God am a jealous God, visiting the iniquity of the fathers upon the children unto the third and fourth generation of them that hate me,*

GOD, IN ALL HIS MAJESTY AND PERFECTION, CANNOT LOOK UPON ANYTHING THAT IS SINFUL. WE ARE ALL SINNERS BECAUSE WE HAVE A SINFUL NATURE INHERITED FROM ADAM.

THAT MEANS THAT NOBODY IN THIS WHOLE UNIVERSE CAN MAKE THEIR WAY TO HEAVEN BY GOOD WORKS, BECAUSE GOD STILL CANNOT LOOK UPON THEM.

OUR GOOD WORKS ARE A STENCH BEFORE GOD.

Isaiah 64:6

> *But we are all as an unclean thing, and all our righteousnesses are as filthy rags; and we all do fade as a leaf; and our iniquities, like the wind, have taken us away.*

Ephesians 2:8-9

> *For by grace are ye saved through faith; and that not of yourselves: it is the gift of God: Not of works, lest any man should boast.*

Romans 3:10

> *As it is written, There is none righteous, no, not one:*

THE TEN COMMANDMENTS WERE GIVEN BY GOD IN ORDER TO SHOW US THAT WE CANNOT KEEP THEM. NONE OF US HAVE LOVED THE LORD OUR GOD WITH <u>ALL</u> OUR HEART, SOUL AND STRENGTH ... GOD WAS REVEALING TO US, THROUGH THESE COMMANDMENTS, THAT WE CANNOT LIVE A PERFECT LIFE WITHOUT SIN, WE ARE ALL SINNERS AND THEREFORE ARE IN NEED OF A SAVIOUR!

GOD WANTS US ALL TO LIVE FOREVER WITH HIM IN HEAVEN. GOD LOVES US UNCONDITIONALLY, AND WANTS A LOVING, PERSONAL RELATIONSHIP WITH US, AND TO GUIDE US INDIVIDUALLY INTO HIS UNIQUE PERFECT PLAN AND DESTINY FOR OUR LIVES. HE IS OUR HEAVENLY FATHER AND THE SPIRIT OF HIS SON, JESUS CHRIST, FLIES INTO OUR HEARTS, CRYING 'ABBA, FATHER'. THE WORD 'ABBA' IS A JEWISH NAME FOR 'DADDY'.

SO GOD DEVISED A PLAN TO RECONCILE US TO HIMSELF, AND REMOVE OUR SIN THAT SEPARATED US FROM HIM:

Isaiah 59:2

> *But your iniquities have separated between you and your God, and your sins have hid his face from you, that he will not hear.*

GOD NEEDED A PERFECT SACRIFICE, WITHOUT BLEMISH, TO PAY THE PRICE FOR OUR SIN. AS THE SCRIPTURE SAYS, *"THERE IS NO-ONE RIGHTEOUS, NO, NOT ONE"*, SO GOD HIMSELF HAD TO BECOME THAT SACRIFICE FOR OUR SIN. HE CAME DOWN FROM HEAVEN AND TOOK UPON HIMSELF A BODY, AND BECAME FLESH.

2 Corinthians 5:19

> *To wit, that God was in Christ, reconciling the world unto himself, not imputing their trespasses unto them;*

John 1:14

> *And the Word was made flesh, and dwelt among us, (and we beheld his glory, the glory as of the only begotten of the Father,) full of grace and truth.*

Hebrews 10:5,6

> *Wherefore when he comes into the world, he says, "Sacrifice and offering thou wouldest not, but a body hast thou prepared me:*

GOD THE SON - JESUS CHRIST,
OUR SAVIOUR, PAID THE
PRICE FOR OUR SINS

John 3:16

> For God so loved the world, that he gave his only begotten Son, that whosoever believeth in him should not perish, but have everlasting life.

2 Corinthians 5:19

> To wit, that God was in Christ, reconciling the world unto himself, not imputing their trespasses unto them; and hath committed unto us the word of reconciliation.

JESUS GAVE HIS LIFE WILLINGLY

John 10:15

> As the Father knoweth me, even so know I the Father: and I lay down my life for the sheep.

2 Corinthians 5:21

> For he hath made him to be sin for us, who knew no sin; that we might be made the righteousness of God in him.

Isaiah 53:10

> Yet it pleased the LORD to bruise him; he hath put him to grief: when thou shalt make his soul an offering for sin, he shall see his seed, he shall prolong his days, and the pleasure of the LORD shall prosper in his hand

John 1:29

> The next day John seeth Jesus coming unto him, and saith, Behold the Lamb of God, which taketh away the sin of the world.

1 Peter 2:24

Who His own self bare our sins in His own body on the tree, that we, being dead to sins, should live unto righteousness: by whose stripes ye were healed.

Galatians 1:4

… our LORD Jesus Christ, who gave Himself for our sins that He might deliver us from this present evil world; according to the will of God and our Father

---

THE LORD JESUS CHRIST PAID THE PRICE FOR OUR SINS WILLINGLY BY BEING CRUCIFIED ON THE CROSS AT CALVARY

Luke 23:34

Then said Jesus, Father, forgive them; for they know not what they do.

JESUS SHED HIS BLOOD IN ORDER THAT WE WOULD BE FORGIVEN BEFORE GOD

Hebrews 9:22

.. without the shedding of blood there is no forgiveness.

WE ARE FORGIVEN BEFORE GOD, THROUGH HIS SON, AND OUR SINS HAVE BEEN PAID FOR!

We can now stand before God, knowing that He can look upon us clothed in the righteousness of His Son,

because Jesus has removed the sin barrier that separated us from the Father.

John 14:6

> *Jesus saith unto him, I am the way, the truth, and the life: no man cometh unto the Father, but by me*

JESUS TOOK OUR SINS IN HIS OWN BODY AND NAILED THEM TO THE CROSS

JESUS PAID THE PENALTY FOR OUR SINS, AND SHED HIS BLOOD FOR OUR FORGIVENESS BEFORE GOD

Romans 6:23

> *For the wages of sin is death; but the gift of God is eternal life through Jesus Christ our Lord.*

Hebrews 9:22

> *And almost all things are by the law purged with blood; and without shedding of blood is no remission.*

1 Peter 3;18

> *Christ also hath once suffered for sins, the just for the unjust, that he might bring us to God, being put to death in the flesh, but quickened by the Spirit:*

1 Peter 2:24

> *Who his own self bare our sins in his own body on the tree, that we, being dead to sins, should live unto righteousness: by whose stripes ye were healed.*

JESUS REMOVED THE 'SIN' BARRIER THAT WAS SEPARATING US FROM GOD. GOD CAN NOW LOOK UPON US JUST AS IF WE HAD NEVER SINNED

John 1:29

The next day John seeth Jesus coming unto him, and saith, Behold the Lamb of God, which taketh away the sin of the world.

Revelation 1:5

…Unto him that loved us, and washed us from our sins in his own blood,

---

THE BIBLE SAYS THERE IS NO OTHER WAY INTO HEAVEN

John 14:6

Jesus saith unto him, I am the way, the truth, and the life: no man cometh unto the Father, but by me.

Matthew 7:13

Enter ye in at the strait gate: for wide is the gate, and broad is the way, that leadeth to destruction, and many there be which go in thereat:

Proverbs 14:12

There is a way which seemeth right unto a man, but the end thereof are the ways of death.

GOD WANTS US ALL TO LIVE FOREVER WITH HIM IN HEAVEN. THE DEVIL WANTS US ALL DEAD RIGHT NOW

Deuteronomy 30:19

> *I call heaven and earth to record this day against you,*
> *that I have set before you life and death, blessing and*
> *cursing: therefore choose life, that both thou and thy*
> *seed may live:*

> *That thou mayest love the LORD thy God, and that*
> *thou mayest obey his voice, and that thou mayest cleave*
> *unto him: for he is thy life, and the length of thy days*

GOD MADE HELL FOR THE DEVIL AND THE DEVIL'S ANGELS

GOD MADE HEAVEN FOR US,
SO THAT WE CAN ALL LIVE FOREVER

THE CHOICE IS OURS!

If you believe in the Lord Jesus Christ
as your Lord and Saviour
say the sinner's prayer on page 130

GOD SAYS:

1 John 5:12

> *He that hath the Son hath life; and he that hath not*
> *the Son of God hath not life.*

THE BEGINNING OF
YOUR NEW LIFE IN CHRIST

REPENT!

**In order to become a Christian we must first repent of all
our sins. Repentance means we are sorry before God, are
turning away from sin, and are changing direction from
our old life, and starting a new life in Christ.**

Acts 2:38

> *Then Peter said unto them, Repent, and be baptized
> every one of you in the name of Jesus Christ for the
> remission of sins, and ye shall receive the gift of the
> Holy Ghost.*

Acts 3:19

> *Repent ye therefore, and be converted, that your sins
> may be blotted out, when the times of refreshing shall
> come from the presence of the Lord.*

2 Peter 3:9

> *The Lord is .. not willing that any should perish, but
> that all should come to repentance.*

QUESTION:

WOULD YOU LIKE TO RECEIVE JESUS CHRIST INTO YOUR HEART AS YOUR PERSONAL SAVIOUR AND LORD?

If so, then please say the following prayer overleaf. If you mean what you say from your heart, God will hear you and you will be saved, because the Bible says:

Romans 10:9
> *That if thou shalt confess with thy mouth the Lord Jesus, and shalt believe in thine heart that God hath raised him from the dead, thou shalt be saved.*

SINNER'S PRAYER

Lord Almighty God

I admit I am a sinner and I need your forgiveness. I believe that Jesus Christ died in my place on the Cross, and paid the penalty for my sins.

I am willing right now to repent and turn away from my sins, and accept Jesus Christ as my personal Saviour and LORD.

I commit myself to You, and ask You to send your Holy Spirit into my life, to fill me and take control, and to help me become the kind of person You want me to be.

Thank You, Father for Loving me, In Jesus' Name,

Amen

YOU ARE NOW A CHILD OF GOD!

John 1:12

But as many as received him, to them gave he power to become the sons of God, even to them that believe on his name:

Romans 10:11

For the scripture saith, Whosoever believeth on him shall not be ashamed.

Romans 10:13

For whosoever shall call upon the name of the Lord shall be saved.

SALVATION IS A FREE GIFT FROM GOD

Romans 6:23

For the wages of sin is death; but the gift of God is eternal life through Jesus Christ our Lord.

WHAT IS YOUR NEXT STEP?

WATER BAPTISM!

BAPTISM IN WATER IS TOTAL IMMERSION; YOU ARE BURYING YOUR PAST SINFUL NATURE

AND RISING UP OUT OF THE WATER WITH

OUR LORD JESUS CHRIST'S NATURE AND HIS RESURRECTION LIFE

Acts 2:38

> *Then Peter said unto them, Repent, and be baptized every one of you in the name of Jesus Christ for the remission of sins, and ye shall receive the gift of the Holy Ghost.*

Colossians 2:12

> *Buried with him in baptism, wherein also ye are risen with him through the faith of the operation of God, who hath raised him from the dead.*

2 Corinthians 5:17

> *Therefore if any man be in Christ, he is a new creature: old things are passed away; behold, all things are become new.*

1 John 5:11

> *And this is the record, that God hath given to us eternal life, and this life is in his Son. He that hath the Son hath life; and he that hath not the Son of God hath not life.*

BABY BAPTISM IS PURELY A DEDICATION BEFORE GOD FOR PROTECTION A BABY CANNOT REPENT OF SIN, OR ACCEPT JESUS AS SAVIOUR!

BIBLICAL EXAMPLES OF WATER BAPTISM

THE LORD JESUS CHRIST

Matthew 3:16

> *And Jesus, when he was baptized, went up straightway out of the water: and, lo, the heavens were opened unto him, and he saw the Spirit of God descending like a dove, and lighting upon him:*

THE ETHIOPIAN EUNUCH

Acts 8:36-39

> *And as they went on their way, they came unto a certain water: and the eunuch said, See, here is water; what doth hinder me to be baptized?*

> *And Philip said, If thou believest with all thine heart, thou mayest. And he answered and said, I believe that Jesus Christ is the Son of God.*

> *And he commanded the chariot to stand still: and they went down both into the water, both Philip and the eunuch; and he baptized him.*

> *And when they were come up out of the water, the Spirit of the Lord caught away Philip, that the eunuch saw him no more: and he went on his way rejoicing.*

SAUL
(WHO BECAME THE APOSTLE PAUL)

Acts 9:18

> *And immediately there fell from his eyes as it had been scales: and he received sight forthwith, and arose, and was baptized.*

CORNELIUS AND HIS HOUSEHOLD

Acts 10:48

> *And he commanded them to be baptized in the name of the Lord. Then prayed they him to tarry certain days.*

THE WATER BAPTISM ALSO <u>EQUIPS</u> YOU FOR GOD'S SERVICE WITH GOD'S GIFTS OF EVANGELIST, PASTOR, TEACHER, APOSTLE OR PROPHET

Ephesians 4:11

> *And He gave some, apostles; and some, prophets; and some, evangelists; and some, pastors and teachers; for the perfecting of the saints for the work of the ministry; for the edifying of the body of Christ.*

SO, NOW YOU HAVE BURIED THE PAST, AND LOOK FORWARD TO GOD'S FUTURE FOR YOU

Question: What will prevent you from going back to your past sinful life?

Answer: The baptism of the Holy Spirit!

Acts 19:6
> *And when Paul had laid his hands upon them, the Holy Ghost came on them; and they spake with tongues, and prophesied.*

BE BAPTISED IN THE HOLY SPIRIT

THE BAPTISM OF THE HOLY SPIRIT IS WHEN GOD THE HOLY SPIRIT FILLS YOU WITH HIS POWER TO HELP YOU TO STOP SINNING, AND YOU ENTER INTO GOD'S PURPOSE, PLAN AND DESTINY FOR YOUR LIFE.

ALSO THE BAPTISM ENABLES YOU TO ENTER INTO AN INTIMATE RELATIONSHIP WITH YOUR HEAVENLY FATHER, 'ABBA' FATHER THROUGH YOUR NEW LIFE IN CHRIST, BY THE POWER OF THE HOLY SPIRIT.

Acts 1:8
> *.. you shall receive power after that the Holy Ghost is come upon you, and ye shall be My witnesses ...*

Matthew 3:16
> *... And he saw the Spirit of God descending like a dove, and alighting on Him [Jesus].*

Matthew 28:18-20

Jesus came and spake unto them, saying, All power is given unto me in heaven and in earth.

Go ye therefore, and teach all nations, baptizing them in the name of the Father, and of the Son, and of the Holy Ghost:

Teaching them to observe all things whatsoever I have commanded you: and, lo, I am with you always, even unto the end of the world. Amen.

John 14:16

And I will pray the Father, and He shall give you another comforter, that He may abide with you forever; even the Spirit of truth; whom the world cannot receive, because it sees Him not, neither knows Him: but we know Him; for He dwells with you, and shall be in you.

John 16:8

And when He is come, He will reprove the world of sin, and of righteousness, and of judgment.

OTHER USEFUL SCRIPTURES FOR EVANGELISM

FROM GENESIS TO REVELATION

(In chronological order)

Genesis 22:17-18
> That in blessing I will bless thee, and in multiplying I will multiply thy seed as the stars of the heaven, and as the sand which is upon the sea shore; and thy seed shall possess the gate of his enemies;
>
> And in thy seed shall all the nations of the earth be blessed; because thou hast obeyed my voice.

Leviticus 17:11 (Hebrews 9:22)
> For the life of the flesh is in the blood: and I have given it to you upon the altar to make an atonement for your souls: for it is the blood that maketh an atonement for the soul.

Hebrews 9:22
> And almost all things are by the law purged with blood; and without shedding of blood is no remission

Leviticus 18:22 (Romans 1:26,27)
> Thou shalt not lie with mankind, as with womankind: it is abomination.

Romans 1:26,27
> For this cause God gave them up unto vile affections: for even their women did change the natural use into that which is against nature:
>
> And likewise also the men, leaving the natural use of the woman, burned in their lust one toward another; men with men working that which is unseemly, and

receiving in themselves that recompence of their error which was meet.

Deuteronomy 8:3(b)

... man doth not live by bread only, but by every word that proceedeth out of the mouth of the LORD doth man live.

Deuteronomy 18: 10-12

There shall not be found among you any one that maketh his son or his daughter to pass through the fire, or that useth divination, or an observer of times, or an enchanter, or a witch. Or a charmer, or a consulter with familiar spirits, or a wizard, or a necromancer. For all that do these things are an abomination unto the LORD: and because of these abominations the LORD thy God doth drive them out from before thee.

Deuteronomy 30:15

See, I have set before thee this day life and good, and death and evil;

In that I command thee this day to love the LORD thy God, to walk in his ways, and to keep his commandments and his statutes and his judgments, that thou mayest live and multiply: and the LORD thy God shall bless thee in the land whither thou goest to possess it.

But if thine heart turn away, so that thou wilt not hear, but shalt be drawn away, and worship other gods, and serve them;

I denounce unto you this day, that ye shall surely perish, and that ye shall not prolong your days upon the land, whither thou passest over Jordan to go to possess it.

I call heaven and earth to record this day against you, that I have set before you life and death, blessing and cursing: therefore choose life, that both thou and thy seed may live:

That thou mayest love the LORD thy God, and that thou mayest obey his voice, and that thou mayest cleave unto him: for he is thy life, and the length of thy days:

Psalms 22:1,18

My God, my God, why hast thou forsaken me?

They part my garments among them, and cast lots upon my vesture.

Psalm 40:7

Then said I, Lo, I come: in the volume of the book it is written of me,

Psalm 68:18

Thou hast ascended on high, thou hast led captivity captive: thou hast received gifts for men; yea, for the rebellious also, that the LORD God might dwell among them.

Psalm 110:1 (Matt 22:24); (Mark 12:36); (Luke 20:42)

The LORD said unto my Lord, Sit thou at my right hand, until I make thine enemies thy footstool.

Psalm 135:15

The idols of the heathen are silver and gold, the work of man's hands. They have mouths, but they speak not; eyes have they, but they see not. They have ears, but they hear not; neither is there any breath in their mouths. They that make them are like unto them.

Proverbs 8:22-36

The LORD possessed me in the beginning of his way, before his works of old.

I was set up from everlasting, from the beginning, or ever the earth was.

When there were no depths, I was brought forth; when there were no fountains abounding with water.

Before the mountains were settled, before the hills was I brought forth:

While as yet he had not made the earth, nor the fields, nor the highest part of the dust of the world.

When he prepared the heavens, I was there: when he set a compass upon the face of the depth:

When he established the clouds above: when he strengthened the fountains of the deep:

When he gave to the sea his decree, that the waters should not pass his commandment: when he appointed the foundations of the earth:

Then I was by him, as one brought up with him: and I was daily his delight, rejoicing always before him;

Rejoicing in the habitable part of his earth; and my delights were with the sons of men.

Now therefore hearken unto me, O ye children: for blessed are they that keep my ways.

Hear instruction, and be wise, and refuse it not.

Blessed is the man that heareth me, watching daily at my gates, waiting at the posts of my doors.

For whoso findeth me findeth life, and shall obtain favour of the LORD.

But he that sinneth against me wrongeth his own soul: all they that hate me love death.

Isaiah 7:14/Matthew 1:23

Therefore the Lord himself shall give you a sign; Behold, a virgin shall conceive, and bear a son, and shall call his name Immanuel.

Isaiah 9:6

For unto us a child is born, unto us a son is given: and the government shall be upon his shoulder: and his name shall be called Wonderful, Counsellor, The mighty God, The everlasting Father, The Prince of Peace.

Isaiah 48:16

Come ye near unto me, hear ye this; I have not spoken in secret from the beginning; from the time that it was, there am I: and now the Lord GOD, and his Spirit, hath sent me.

Isaiah 52:14-15

So shall He sprinkle any nations; the kings shall shut their mouths at Him: for that which had not been told them shall they see; and that which they had not heard shall they consider.

Isaiah 53:5-12

But he was wounded for our transgressions, he was bruised for our iniquities: the chastisement of our peace was upon him; and with his stripes we are healed.

All we like sheep have gone astray; we have turned every one to his own way; and the LORD hath laid on him the iniquity of us all.

He was oppressed, and he was afflicted, yet he opened not his mouth: he is brought as a lamb to the slaughter, and as a sheep before her shearers is dumb, so he openeth not his mouth.

He was taken from prison and from judgment: and who shall declare his generation? for he was cut off out of the land of the living: for the transgression of my people was he stricken.

And he made his grave with the wicked, and with the rich in his death; because he had done no violence, neither was any deceit in his mouth.

Yet it pleased the LORD to bruise him; he hath put him to grief: when thou shalt make his soul an offering for sin, he shall see his seed, he shall prolong his days, and the pleasure of the LORD shall prosper in his hand.

*He shall see of the travail of his soul, and shall be
satisfied: by his knowledge shall my righteous servant
justify many; for he shall bear their iniquities.*

*Therefore will I divide him a portion with the great,
and he shall divide the spoil with the strong; because
he hath poured out his soul unto death: and he was
numbered with the transgressors; and he bare the sin of
many, and made intercession for the transgressors.*

Isaiah 59:2

*But your iniquities have separated between you and
your God, and your sins have hid his face from you,
that he will not hear.*

Isaiah 60:12

*For the nation and kingdom that will not serve thee
shall perish; yea, those nations shall be utterly wasted.*

Isaiah 64:6

*But we are all as an unclean thing, and all our
righteousnesses are as filthy rags; and we all do fade as
a leaf; and our iniquities, like the wind, have taken
us away.*

Jeremiah 23:29

*Is not my word like as a fire? says the LORD; and like
a hammer that breaks the rock in pieces?*

Zechariah 9:9

*Rejoice greatly, O daughter of Zion; shout, O daughter
of Jerusalem: behold, thy King cometh unto thee: he is*

just, and having salvation; lowly, and riding upon an ass, and upon a colt the foal of an ass.

Zechariah 11:12

And I said unto them, If ye think good, give me my price; and if not, forbear. So they weighed for my price thirty pieces of silver.

Zechariah 12:10

And I will pour upon the house of David, and upon the inhabitants of Jerusalem, the spirit of grace and of supplications: and they shall look upon me whom they have pierced, and they shall mourn for him, as one mourneth for his only son, and shall be in bitterness for him, as one that is in bitterness for his firstborn.

Zechariah 14

Behold, THE day of the LORD cometh, and thy spoil shall be divided in the midst of thee.

For I will gather all nations against Jerusalem to battle; and the city shall be taken, and the houses rifled, the women ravished; and half of the city shall go forth into captivity, and the residue of the people shall not be cut off from the city.

Then shall the LORD go forth, and fight against those nations, as when He fought in the day of battle.

And His feet shall stand in that day upon the mount of Olives, which is before Jerusalem on the east, and the mount of Olives shall cleave in the midst thereof toward the east and toward the west, and there shall be a very great valley; and half of the mountain shall remove toward the north, and half of it toward the south.

And ye shall flee to the valley of the mountains. For the valley of the mountains shall reach unto Azal: yea, ye shall flee, like as ye fled from before the earthquake in the day of Uzziah king of Judah: and the LORD my God shall come and all the saints with thee.

And it shall come to pass in that day that the light shall not be clear, nor dark:

But it shall be one which shall be known to the LORD, not day, nor night, but it shall come to pass, that at evening time it shall be light.

And it shall be in that day, that living waters shall go out from Jerusalem; half of them toward the former sea, and half of them toward the hinder sea: in summer and in winter shall it be.

And the LORD shall be king over all the earth: in that day shall there be one LORD, and His name one.

All the land shall be turned as a plain from Geba to Rimmon south of Jerusalem: and it shall be lifted up, and inhabited in her place, from

Benjamin's gate unto the place of the first gate, unto the corner gate, and from the tower of Hananeel unto the king's winepresses.

And men shall dwell in it, and there shall be no more utter destruction; but Jerusalem shall be safely inhabited.

Micah 5:2

But thou, Bethlehem Ephratah, though thou be little among the thousands of Judah, yet out of thee shall He come forth unto me that is to be ruler in Israel; whose goings forth have been from of old, from everlasting.

Malachi 4

But in the last days it shall come to pass, that the mountain of the house of the LORD shall be established in the top of the mountains, and it shall be exalted above the hills; and people shall flow unto it.

And many nations shall come, and say, Come, and let us go up to the mountain of the LORD, and to the house of the God of Jacob; and he will teach us of his ways, and we will walk in his paths: for the law shall go forth of Zion, and the word of the LORD from Jerusalem.

And he shall judge among many people, and rebuke strong nations afar off; and they shall beat their swords into plowshares, and their spears into pruninghooks: nation shall not lift up a sword against nation, neither shall they learn war any more.

But they shall sit every man under his vine and under his fig tree; and none shall make them afraid: for the mouth of the LORD of hosts hath spoken it.

BOOK OF MATTHEW

Matthew 1:21-23 [Isaiah 7:14]

And she shall bring forth a son, and thou shalt call his name JESUS: for he shall save his people from their sins.

Now all this was done, that it might be fulfilled which was spoken of the Lord by the prophet, saying,

Behold, a virgin shall be with child, and shall bring forth a son, and they shall call his name Emmanuel, which being interpreted is, God with us.

Matthew 9:6

But that ye may know that the Son of man hath power on earth to forgive sins, (then saith he to the sick of the palsy,) Arise, take up thy bed, and go unto thine house.

Matthew 10:32

Whosoever therefore shall confess me before men, him will I confess also before my Father which is in heaven.

Matthew 11:28

Come unto Me, all you that labour and are heavy laden, and I will give you rest. Take my yoke and learn of Me; for I am meek and lowly in heart: and you shall find rest for your souls. For my yoke is easy and my burden is light.

Matthew 12:50

For whosoever shall do the will of My Father which is in Heaven, the same is my brother, and sister, and mother.

Matthew 13:40

..so shall it be in the end of this world. The Son of man shall send forth His angels and they shall gather out of His kingdom all things that offend .. and shall cast them into a furnace of fire ..

Matthew 15:25

Then came she and worshipped Him ...

Matthew 16:27

For the Son of man shall come in the glory of His Father with His angels; and then shall He reward every man according to his works.

Matthew 17:2,3

Jesus was transfigured ... there appeared unto them Moses and Elijah talking with Him.

Matthew 20:28

Even as the Son of man came not to be ministered unto, but to minister, and to give His life a ransom for many.

Matthew 24:35

Heaven and earth shall pass away but My words shall not pass away

Matthew 24:14

And this gospel of the kingdom shall be preached in all the world for a witness unto all nations; and then shall the end come.

Matthew 26:24

The Son of man goeth as it is written of Him: ...

Psalm 22

They part my garments among them, and cast lots upon my vesture.

Isaiah 53

But he was wounded for our transgressions, he was bruised for our iniquities: the chastisement of our peace was upon him; and with his stripes we are healed.

Daniel 9:26

And after threescore and two weeks shall Messiah be cut off, but not for himself: and the people of the prince that shall come shall destroy the city and the sanctuary; and the end thereof shall be with a flood, and unto the end of the war desolations are determined.

Mark 9:12

And he answered and told them, Elias verily cometh first, and restoreth all things; and how it is written of the Son of man, that he must suffer many things, and be set at nought.

Luke 24:25

Then he said unto them, O fools, and slow of heart to believe all that the prophets have spoken:

Luke 24:46

And said unto them, Thus it is written, and thus it behooved Christ to suffer, and to rise from the dead the third day:

Acts 17:2,3

And Paul, as his manner was, went in unto them, and three sabbath days reasoned with them out of the scriptures,

Opening and alleging, that Christ must needs have suffered, and risen again from the dead; and that this Jesus, whom I preach unto you, is Christ.

Acts 26:22,23

Having therefore obtained help of God, I continue unto this day, witnessing both to small and great, saying none other things than those which the prophets and Moses did say should come:

That Christ should suffer, and that he should be the first that should rise from the dead, and should shew light unto the people, and to the Gentiles.

1 Corinthians 15:3

For I delivered unto you first of all that which I also received, how that Christ died for our sins according to the scriptures;

Matthew 26:28

For this is my blood of the new testament, which is shed for many for the remission of sins.

Matthew 28:18-20

And Jesus came and spake unto them, saying, All power is given unto me in heaven and in earth.

Go ye therefore, and teach all nations, baptizing them in the name of the Father, and of the Son, and of the Holy Ghost:

Teaching them to observe all things whatsoever I have commanded you: and, lo, I am with you always, even unto the end of the world. Amen.

BOOK OF MARK

Mark 1:15 *[Jesus speaking]*
.. *repent and believe the Gospel*

Mark 2:10
... *that you may know that the Son of man has power on earth to forgive sins*

Mark 10:45
.. *the Son of man came not to be ministered unto,*

Mark 13:31
Heaven and earth will pass away: but my words shall not pass away

Mark 16:15,16
And he said unto them,

Go ye into all the world, and preach the gospel to every creature.

He that believeth and is baptized shall be saved; but he that believeth not shall be damned.

BOOK OF LUKE

Luke 2:11

For unto you is born this day in the city of David a Saviour, which is Christ the Lord.

Luke 3:16

John answered, saying unto them all, I indeed baptize you with water; but one mightier than I cometh, the latchet of whose shoes I am not worthy to unloose: he shall baptize you with the Holy Ghost and with fire:

Luke 5:24

But that ye may know that the Son of man hath power upon earth to forgive sins, (he said unto the sick of the palsy,) I say unto thee, Arise, and take up thy couch, and go into thine house.

Luke 9:28-31

And it came to pass about an eight days after these sayings, he took Peter and John and James, and went up into a mountain to pray.

And as he prayed, the fashion of his countenance was altered, and his raiment was white and glistering.

And, behold, there talked with him two men, which were Moses and Elias:

Who appeared in glory, and spake of his decease which he should accomplish at Jerusalem.

Margaret F. Blanchon

Luke 13:5 *[Jesus speaking]*
.. except you repent, you shall all likewise perish

Luke 24:44
And he said unto them, These are the words which I spake unto you, while I was yet with you, that all things must be fulfilled, which were written in the law of Moses, and in the prophets, and in the psalms, concerning me.

Luke 24:46 *[Jesus, after His resurrection]*
And said unto them,

Thus it is written, and thus it behooved Christ to suffer, and to rise from the dead the third day:

And that repentance and remission of sins should be preached in his name among all nations, beginning at Jerusalem.

BOOK OF JOHN

John 1:1-4

In the beginning was the Word, and the Word was with God, and the Word was God.

The same was in the beginning with God.

All things were made by him; and without him was not any thing made that was made.

In him was life; and the life was the light of men.

John 1:12

But as many as received him, to them gave he power to become the sons of God, even to them that believe on his name:

John 1:14

And the Word was made flesh, and dwelt among us, (and we beheld his glory, the glory as of the only begotten of the Father,) full of grace and truth.

John 1:29

The next day John seeth Jesus coming unto him, and saith, Behold the Lamb of God, which taketh away the sin of the world.

John 1:34-36

And I saw, and bare record that this is the Son of God.

Again the next day after John stood, and two of his disciples;

And looking upon Jesus as he walked, he saith, Behold the Lamb of God!

John 3:3-7

Jesus answered and said unto him, Verily, verily, I say unto thee, Except a man be born again, he cannot see the kingdom of God.

Nicodemus saith unto him, How can a man be born when he is old? can he enter the second time into his mother's womb, and be born?

Jesus answered, Verily, verily, I say unto thee, Except a man be born of water and of the Spirit, he cannot enter into the kingdom of God.

That which is born of the flesh is flesh; and that which is born of the Spirit is spirit.

Marvel not that I said unto thee, Ye must be born again.

John 3:14-18

And as Moses lifted up the serpent in the wilderness, even so must the Son of man be lifted up:

That whosoever believeth in him should not perish, but have eternal life.

For God so loved the world, that he gave his only begotten Son, that whosoever believeth in him should not perish, but have everlasting life.

For God sent not his Son into the world to condemn the world; but that the world through him might be saved.

He that believeth on him is not condemned: but he that believeth not is condemned already, because he hath not believed in the name of the only begotten Son of God.

John 5:39

Search the scriptures; for in them ye think ye have eternal life: and they are they which testify of me.

John 5:46

For had ye believed Moses, ye would have believed me; for he wrote of me.

John 6:33

For the bread of God is he which cometh down from heaven, and giveth life unto the world.

John 6:47-51

Verily, verily, I say unto you, He that believeth on me hath everlasting life.

I am that bread of life.

Your fathers did eat manna in the wilderness, and are dead.

This is the bread which cometh down from heaven, that a man may eat thereof, and not die.

I am the living bread which came down from heaven: if any man eat of this bread, he shall live for ever: and the bread that I will give is my flesh, which I will give for the life of the world.

John 7:38

He that believeth on me, as the scripture hath said, out of his belly shall flow rivers of living water.

John 8:12

Then spake Jesus again unto them, saying, I am the light of the world: he that followeth me shall not walk in darkness, but shall have the light of life.

John 8:23

And he said unto them, Ye are from beneath; I am from above: ye are of this world; I am not of this world.

John 8:51

Verily, verily, I say unto you, If a man keep my saying, he shall never see death.

John 8:56

Your father Abraham rejoiced to see my day: and he saw it, and was glad.

John 8:58

Jesus said unto them, Verily, verily, I say unto you, Before Abraham was, I am.

Exodus 3:14

And God said unto Moses, I AM THAT I AM: and he said, Thus shalt thou say unto the children of Israel, I AM hath sent me unto you.

John 9:5

> As long as I am in the world, I am the light of the world.

John 10:9

> I am the door: by me if any man enter in, he shall be saved, and shall go in and out, and find pasture.

John 10:15

> As the Father knoweth me, even so know I the Father: and I lay down my life for the sheep.

John 10:27,28

> My sheep hear my voice, and I know them, and they follow me: And I give unto them eternal life; and they shall never perish, neither shall any man pluck them out of my hand.

John 10:30

> I and my Father are one.

John 11:25,26

> Jesus said unto her, I am the resurrection, and the life: he that believeth in me, though he were dead, yet shall he live:And whosoever liveth and believeth in me shall never die. Believest thou this?

John 12:32

> And I, if I be lifted up from the earth, will draw all men unto me.

John 12:46-48

I am come a light into the world, that whosoever believeth on me should not abide in darkness.

And if any man hear my words, and believe not, I judge him not: for I came not to judge the world, but to save the world.

He that rejecteth me, and receiveth not my words, hath one that judgeth him: the word that I have spoken, the same shall judge him in the last day.

John 14:6

Jesus saith unto him, I am the way, the truth, and the life: no man cometh unto the Father, but by me.

John 14:13

And whatsoever ye shall ask in my name, that will I do, that the Father may be glorified in the Son.

John 15:1

I am the true vine, and my Father is the husbandman.

John 15:13

Greater love hath no man than this, that a man lay down his life for his friends.

John 20:31

But these are written, that ye might believe that Jesus is the Christ, the Son of God; and that believing ye might have life through his name.

BOOK OF ACTS

Acts 2:21

And it shall come to pass, that whosoever shall call on the name of the Lord shall be saved.

Romans 10:13

For whosoever shall call upon the name of the Lord shall be saved.

Acts 3:19-21

Repent ye therefore, and be converted, that your sins may be blotted out, when the times of refreshing shall come from the presence of the Lord.

And he shall send Jesus Christ, which before was preached unto you:

Whom the heaven must receive until the times of restitution of all things, which God hath spoken by the mouth of all his holy prophets since the world began.

Acts 3:26

Unto you first God, having raised up his Son Jesus, sent him to bless you, in turning away every one of you from his iniquities.

Acts 4:12

Neither is there salvation in any other: for there is none other name under heaven given among men, whereby we must be saved.

Acts 5:31

Him hath God exalted with his right hand to be a Prince and a Saviour, for to give repentance to Israel, and forgiveness of sins.

Acts 8:37

And Philip said, If thou believest with all thine heart, thou mayest. And he answered and said, I believe that Jesus Christ is the Son of God.

Acts 9:18

And immediately there fell from his eyes as it had been scales: and he received sight forthwith, and arose, and was baptized.

Acts 10:42,43

And he commanded us to preach unto the people, and to testify that it is he which was ordained of God to be the Judge of quick and dead.

To him give all the prophets witness, that through his name whosoever believeth in him shall receive remission of sins.

Acts 13:38

Be it known unto you therefore, men and brethren, that through this man is preached unto you the forgiveness of sins:

Acts 16:30,31

And brought them out, and said, Sirs, what must I do to be saved? And they said, Believe on the Lord Jesus Christ, and thou shalt be saved, and thy house.

Acts 17:30,31

> *And the times of this ignorance God winked at; but now commandeth all men every where to repent:*
>
> *Because he hath appointed a day, in the which he will judge the world in righteousness by that man whom he hath ordained;*
>
> *whereof he hath given assurance unto all men, in that he hath raised him from the dead.*

BOOK OF ROMANS

Romans 2:16

In the day when God shall judge the secrets of men by Jesus Christ according to my Gospel

Romans 3:23,24

For all have sinned, and come short of the glory of God; being justified freely by his grace through the redemption that is in Christ Jesus:

Romans 5:1

Therefore being justified by faith, we have peace with God through our Lord Jesus Christ

Romans 5:8-10

But God commendeth his love toward us, in that, while we were yet sinners, Christ died for us.

Much more then, being now justified by his blood, we shall be saved from wrath through him.

For if, when we were enemies, we were reconciled to God by the death of his Son, much more, being reconciled, we shall be saved by his life.

Romans 5:12

Wherefore, as by one man sin entered into the world, and death by sin; and so death passed upon all men, for that all have sinned:

Romans 6:4-5

Therefore we are buried with him by baptism into death: that like as Christ was raised up from the dead by the glory of the Father, even so we also should walk in newness of life. For if we have been planted together in the likeness of his death, we shall be also in the likeness of his resurrection:

Romans 6:23

For the wages of sin is death; but the gift of God is eternal life through Jesus Christ our Lord.

Romans 10:9-12

That if thou shalt confess with thy mouth the Lord Jesus, and shalt believe in thine heart that God hath raised him from the dead, thou shalt be saved.

For with the heart man believeth unto righteousness; and with the mouth confession is made unto salvation.

For the scripture saith, Whosoever believeth on him shall not be ashamed.

For there is no difference between the Jew and the Greek: for the same Lord over all is rich unto all that call upon him.

For whosoever shall call upon the name of the Lord shall be saved.

Romans 10:17

So then faith cometh by hearing, and hearing by the word of God.

Margaret F. Blanchon

Romans 14:8

For whether we live, we live unto the Lord; and whether we die, we die unto the Lord: whether we live therefore, or die, we are the Lord's.

Romans 14:10 / 2 Cor 5:10

But why dost thou judge thy brother? or why dost thou set at nought thy brother? for we shall all stand before the judgment seat of Christ.

Romans 14:11-12 / Isaiah 45:23

For it is written, As I live, says the LORD, every knee shall bow to Me, and every tongue confess to God. So then every one of us shall give account of himself to God.

Romans 14:17

... the Kingdom of God is ... righteousness, peace, and joy in the Holy Ghost

Romans 15:6

... God, the Father of Jesus Christ

BOOK OF 1 CORINTHIANS

1 Corinthians 1: 18-21

For the preaching of the cross is to them that perish foolishness; but unto us which are saved it is the power of God.

For it is written, I will destroy the wisdom of the wise, and will bring to nothing the understanding of the prudent.

Where is the wise? where is the scribe? where is the disputer of this world? hath not God made foolish the wisdom of this world?

For after that in the wisdom of God the world by wisdom knew not God, it pleased God by the foolishness of preaching to save them that believe.

1 Corinthians 9:14

Even so hath the Lord ordained that they which preach the gospel should live of the gospel.

1 Corinthians 15:3-12

For I delivered unto you first of all that which I also received, how that Christ died for our sins according to the scriptures;

And that he was buried, and that he rose again the third day according to the scriptures:

And that he was seen of Cephas, then of the twelve:

After that, he was seen of above five hundred brethren at once; of whom the greater part remain unto this present, but some are fallen asleep.

After that, he was seen of James; then of all the apostles.

And last of all he was seen of me also, as of one born out of due time.

For I am the least of the apostles, that am not meet to be called an apostle, because I persecuted the church of God.

1 Corinthians 15:20

But now is Christ risen from the dead, and become the firstfruits of them that slept.

1 Corinthians 15:23-28

But every man in his own order: Christ the firstfruits; afterward they that are Christ's at his coming.

Then cometh the end, when he shall have delivered up the kingdom to God, even the Father; when he shall have put down all rule and all authority and power.

For he must reign, till he hath put all enemies under his feet.

The last enemy that shall be destroyed is death.

For he hath put all things under his feet. But when he saith all things are put under him, it is manifest that he is excepted, which did put all things under him.

And when all things shall be subdued unto him, then shall the Son also himself be subject unto him that put all things under him, that God may be all in all.

1 Corinthians 15:51-54

Behold, I shew you a mystery; We shall not all sleep, but we shall all be changed,

In a moment, in the twinkling of an eye, at the last trump: for the trumpet shall sound, and the dead shall be raised incorruptible, and we shall be changed.

For this corruptible must put on incorruption, and this mortal must put on immortality.

So when this corruptible shall have put on incorruption, and this mortal shall have put on immortality, then shall be brought to pass the saying that is written, Death is swallowed up in victory.

BOOK OF 2 CORINTHIANS

2 Corinthians 5:10

For we must all appear before the judgment seat of Christ; that every one may receive the things done in his body, according to that he hath done, whether it be good or bad.

2 Corinthians 5:17

Therefore if any man be in Christ, he is a new creature: old things are passed away; behold, all things are become new.

2 Corinthians 5:18

And all things are of God, who hath reconciled us to himself by Jesus Christ, and hath given to us the ministry of reconciliation;

2 Corinthians 5:21

For he hath made him to be sin for us, who knew no sin; that we might be made the righteousness of God in him.

2 Corinthians 6:2

(For he saith, I have heard thee in a time accepted, and in the day of salvation have I succoured thee: behold, now is the accepted time; behold, now is the day of salvation.)

BOOK OF GALATIANS

Galatians 1:3-4

Grace be to you and peace from God the Father, and from our Lord Jesus Christ, who gave himself for our sins, that he might deliver us from this present evil world, according to the will of God and our Father:

BOOK OF EPHESIANS

Ephesians 1:7

In whom we have redemption through his blood, the forgiveness of sins, according to the riches of his grace;

Ephesians 1:20,21

And what is the exceeding greatness of his power to us-ward who believe, according to the working of his mighty power,

Which he wrought in Christ, when he raised him from the dead, and set him at his own right hand in the heavenly places,

Far above all principality, and power, and might, and dominion, and every name that is named, not only in this world, but also in that which is to come:

And hath put all things under his feet, and gave him to be the head over all things to the church,

Which is his body, the fulness of him that filleth all in all.

Ephesians 2:6

And hath raised us up together, and made us sit together in heavenly places in Christ Jesus:

Ephesians 2:8-9

For by grace are ye saved through faith; and that not of yourselves: it is the gift of God:

Not of works, lest any man should boast.

Ephesians 5:2

And walk in love, as Christ also hath loved us, and hath given himself for us an offering and a sacrifice to God for a sweet smelling savour.

BOOK OF PHILIPPIANS

Philippians 2:9-11

Wherefore God also hath highly exalted him, and given him a name which is above every name:

That at the name of Jesus every knee should bow, of things in heaven, and things in earth, and things under the earth;

And that every tongue should confess that Jesus Christ is Lord, to the glory of God the Father.

BOOK OF COLOSSIANS

Colossians 1:13-21

Who hath delivered us from the power of darkness, and hath translated us into the kingdom of his dear Son:

In whom we have redemption through his blood, even the forgiveness of sins:

Who is the image of the invisible God, the firstborn of every creature:

For by him were all things created, that are in heaven, and that are in earth, visible and invisible, whether they be thrones, or dominions, or principalities, or powers: all things were created by him, and for him:

And he is before all things, and by him all things consist.

And he is the head of the body, the church: who is the beginning, the firstborn from the dead; that in all things he might have the preeminence.

For it pleased the Father that in him should all fulness dwell;

And, having made peace through the blood of his cross, by him to reconcile all things unto himself; by him, I say, whether they be things in earth, or things in heaven.

And you, that were sometime alienated and enemies in your mind by wicked works, yet now hath he reconciled

Colossians 2:9-10

For in him dwelleth all the fulness of the Godhead bodily.

And ye are complete in him, which is the head of all principality and power:

Colossians 2:12-15

Buried with him in baptism, wherein also ye are risen with him through the faith of the operation of God, who hath raised him from the dead.

And you, being dead in your sins and the uncircumcision of your flesh, hath he quickened together with him, having forgiven you all trespasses;

Blotting out the handwriting of ordinances that was against us, which was contrary to us, and took it out of the way, nailing it to his cross;

And having spoiled principalities and powers, he made a shew of them openly, triumphing over them in it.

Colossians 3:1-3

If ye then be risen with Christ, seek those things which are above, where Christ sitteth on the right hand of God.

Set your affection on things above, not on things on the earth.

For ye are dead, and your life is hid with Christ in God.

BOOK OF 1 THESSALONIANS

1 Thessalonians 1:10

And to wait for his Son from heaven, whom he raised from the dead, even Jesus, which delivered us from the wrath to come.

Margaret F. Blanchon

BOOK OF 2 THESSALONIANS

2 Thessalonians 1:7-9

And to you who are troubled rest with us, when the Lord Jesus shall be revealed from heaven with his mighty angels,

In flaming fire taking vengeance on them that know not God, and that obey not the gospel of our Lord Jesus Christ:

Who shall be punished with everlasting destruction from the presence of the Lord, and from the glory of his power;

2 Thessalonians 2:8

And then shall that Wicked be revealed, whom the Lord shall consume with the spirit of his mouth, and shall destroy with the brightness of his coming:

BOOK OF 1 TIMOTHY

1 Timothy 1:15

This is a faithful saying, and worthy of all acceptation, that Christ Jesus came into the world to save sinners; of whom I am chief.

1 Timothy 2:5-6

For there is one God, and one mediator between God and men, the man Christ Jesus; who gave himself a ransom for all, to be testified in due time.

1 Timothy 3:16

And without controversy great is the mystery of godliness: God was manifest in the flesh, justified in the Spirit, seen of angels, preached unto the Gentiles, believed on in the world, received up into glory.

BOOK OF TITUS

Titus 2:13-14

Looking for that blessed hope, and the glorious appearing of the great God and our Saviour Jesus Christ;

Who gave himself for us, that he might redeem us from all iniquity, and purify unto himself a peculiar people, zealous of good works.

Titus 3:4-5

But after that the kindness and love of God our Saviour toward man appeared, Not by works of righteousness which we have done, but according to his mercy he saved us, by the washing of regeneration, and renewing of the Holy Ghost;

BOOK OF HEBREWS

Hebrews 1:1-3

God, who at sundry times and in divers manners spake in time past unto the fathers by the prophets,

Hath in these last days spoken unto us by his Son, whom he hath appointed heir of all things, by whom also he made the worlds;

Who being the brightness of his glory, and the express image of his person, and upholding all things by the word of his power, when he had by himself purged our sins, sat down on the right hand of the Majesty on high:

Hebrews 2:9

But we see Jesus, who was made a little lower than the angels for the suffering of death, crowned with glory and honour; that he by the grace of God should taste death for every man.

Hebrews 2:14

Forasmuch then as the children are partakers of flesh and blood, he also himself likewise took part of the same; that through death he might destroy him that had the power of death, that is, the devil;

And deliver them who through fear of death were all their lifetime subject to bondage.

Hebrews 9:22

And almost all things are by te law purged with blood; and without shedding of blood is no remission.

Hebrews 9:26-28

For then must he often have suffered since the foundation of the world: but now once in the end of the world hath he appeared to put away sin by the sacrifice of himself.

And as it is appointed unto men once to die, but after this the judgment:

So Christ was once offered to bear the sins of many; and unto them that look for him shall he appear the second time without sin unto salvation.

Hebrews 10:12

But this man, after he had offered one sacrifice for sins for ever, sat down on the right hand of God;

Hebrews 12:14

Follow peace with all men, and holiness, without which no man shall see the Lord:

Hebrews 13:8

Jesus Christ the same yesterday, and to day, and for ever.

Hebrews 13:20

Now the God of peace, that brought again from the dead our Lord Jesus, that great shepherd of the sheep, through the blood of the everlasting covenant,

BOOK OF 1 PETER

1 Peter 1:18-20

Forasmuch as ye know that ye were not redeemed with corruptible things, as silver and gold, from your vain conversation received by tradition from your fathers;

But with the precious blood of Christ, as of a lamb without blemish and without spot:

Who verily was foreordained before the foundation of the world, but was manifest in these last times for you,

1 Peter 2:24

Who his own self bare our sins in his own body on the tree, that we, being dead to sins, should live unto righteousness: by whose stripes ye were healed.

BOOK OF 2 PETER

2 Peter 1:21

For the prophecy came not in old time by the will of man: but holy men of God spake as they were moved by the Holy Ghost.

BOOK OF 1 JOHN

1 John 3:8

He that committeth sin is of the devil; for the devil sinneth from the beginning. For this purpose the Son of God was manifested, that he might destroy the works of the devil.

1 John 4:9

In this was manifested the love of God toward us, because that God sent his only begotten Son into the world, that we might live through him.

1 John 4:14,15

And we have seen and do testify that the Father sent the Son to be the Saviour of the world.

Whosoever shall confess that Jesus is the Son of God, God dwelleth in him, and he in God.

1 John 5:1

Whosoever believeth that Jesus is the Christ is born of God: and every one that loveth him that begat loveth him also that is begotten of him.

1 John 5:5

Who is he that overcometh the world, but he that believeth that Jesus is the Son of God?

1 John 5:11-13

And this is the record, that God hath given to us eternal life, and this life is in his Son. He that hath the Son hath life; and he that hath not the Son of God hath not life. These things have I written unto you that believe on the name of the Son of God; that ye may know that ye have eternal life, and that ye may believe on the name of the Son of God.

BOOK OF 2 JOHN

2 John 1:9

Whosoever transgresseth, and abideth not in the doctrine of Christ, hath not God. He that abideth in the doctrine of Christ, he hath both the Father and the Son.

BOOK OF REVELATION

Revelation 1:5

And from Jesus Christ, who is the faithful witness, and the first begotten of the dead, and the prince of the kings of the earth. Unto him that loved us, and washed us from our sins in his own blood,

Revelation 1:7-8

Behold, he cometh with clouds; and every eye shall see him, and they also which pierced him: and all kindreds of the earth shall wail because of him. Even so, Amen.

I am Alpha and Omega, the beginning and the ending, saith the Lord, which is, and which was, and which is to come, the Almighty.

Revelation 1:18

I am he that liveth, and was dead; and, behold, I am alive for evermore, Amen; and have the keys of hell and of death.

Revelation 3:5

He that overcometh, the same shall be clothed in white raiment; and I will not blot out his name out of the book of life, but I will confess his name before my Father, and before his angels.

Revelation 3:20

Behold, I stand at the door, and knock: if any man hear my voice, and open the door, I will come in to him, and will sup with him, and he with me.

Revelation 19:13

And I saw heaven opened, and behold a white horse; and he that sat upon him was called Faithful and True, and in righteousness he doth judge and make war.

His eyes were as a flame of fire, and on his head were many crowns; and he had a name written, that no man knew, but he himself.

And he was clothed with a vesture dipped in blood: and his name is called The Word of God.

And the armies which were in heaven followed him upon white horses, clothed in fine linen, white and clean.

And out of his mouth goeth a sharp sword, that with it he should smite the nations: and he shall rule them with a rod of iron: and he treadeth the winepress of the fierceness and wrath of Almighty God.

And he hath on his vesture and on his thigh a name written, KING OF KINGS, AND LORD OF LORDS.

Revelation 20:11-15

And I saw a great white throne, and him that sat on it, from whose face the earth and the heaven fled away; and there was found no place for them.

And I saw the dead, small and great, stand before God; and the books were opened: and another book was opened, which is the book of life: and the dead were judged out of those things which were written in the books, according to their works.

And the sea gave up the dead which were in it; and death and hell delivered up the dead which were in them: and they were judged every man according to their works.

And death and hell were cast into the lake of fire. This is the second death.

And whosoever was not found written in the book of life was cast into the lake of fire.

Revelation 21:6-7

And he said unto me, It is done. I am Alpha and Omega, the beginning and the end. I will give unto him that is athirst of the fountain of the water of life freely.

He that overcometh shall inherit all things; and I will be his God, and he shall be my son.

ONE-PAGE WITNESSING

ONE-PAGE WITNESSING

Matthew 25:31

When the Son of man shall come in his glory, and all the holy angels with him, then shall he sit upon the throne of his glory:

And before him shall be gathered all nations: and he shall separate them one from another, as a shepherd divideth his sheep from the goats:

ONE-PAGE WITNESSING

Matthew 28:18-20

And Jesus came and spake unto them, saying, All power is given unto me in heaven and in earth.

Go ye therefore, and teach all nations, baptizing them in the name of the Father, and of the Son, and of the Holy Ghost:

Teaching them to observe all things whatsoever I have commanded you: and, lo, I am with you always, even unto the end of the world. Amen.

ONE-PAGE WITNESSING

Luke 4:16-21

And he came to Nazareth, where he had been brought up: and, as his custom was, he went into the synagogue on the sabbath day, and stood up for to read.

And there was delivered unto him the book of the prophet Esaias. And when he had opened the book, he found the place where it was written,

The Spirit of the Lord is upon me, because he hath anointed me to preach the gospel to the poor; he hath sent me to heal the brokenhearted, to preach deliverance to the captives, and recovering of sight to the blind, to set at liberty them that are bruised,

To preach the acceptable year of the Lord.

And he closed the book, and he gave it again to the minister, and sat down. And the eyes of all them that were in the synagogue were fastened on him.

And he began to say unto them,

This day is this scripture fulfilled in your ears.

ONE-PAGE WITNESSING

Even the devils knew that Jesus was the Christ

Luke 4:31-41

And came down to Capernaum, a city of Galilee, and taught them on the sabbath days.

And they were astonished at his doctrine: for his word was with power.

And in the synagogue there was a man, which had a spirit of an unclean devil, and cried out with a loud voice,

Saying, Let us alone; what have we to do with thee, thou Jesus of Nazareth? art thou come to destroy us? I know thee who thou art; the Holy One of God.

And Jesus rebuked him, saying, Hold thy peace, and come out of him. And when the devil had thrown him in the midst, he came out of him, and hurt him not.

And they were all amazed, and spake among themselves, saying, What a word is this! for with authority and power he commandeth the unclean spirits, and they come out.

And the fame of him went out into every place of the country round about.

And he arose out of the synagogue, and entered into Simon's house. And Simon's wife's mother was taken with a great fever; and they besought him for her.

And he stood over her, and rebuked the fever; and it left her: and immediately she arose and ministered unto them.

Now when the sun was setting, all they that had any sick with divers diseases brought them unto him; and he laid his hands on every one of them, and healed them.

And devils also came out of many, crying out, and saying, Thou art Christ the Son of God. And he rebuking them suffered them not to speak: for they knew that he was Christ.

ONE-PAGE WITNESSING

Luke 24:25-53

Then he said unto them, O fools, and slow of heart to believe all that the prophets have spoken:

Ought not Christ to have suffered these things, and to enter into his glory?

And beginning at Moses and all the prophets, he expounded unto them in all the scriptures the things concerning himself.

And they drew nigh unto the village, whither they went: and he made as though he would have gone further.

But they constrained him, saying, Abide with us: for it is toward evening, and the day is far spent. And he went in to tarry with them.

And it came to pass, as he sat at meat with them, he took bread, and blessed it, and brake, and gave to them.

And their eyes were opened, and they knew him; and he vanished out of their sight.

And they said one to another, Did not our heart burn within us, while he talked with us by the way, and while he opened to us the scriptures?

And they rose up the same hour, and returned to Jerusalem, and found the eleven gathered together, and them that were with them,

Saying, The Lord is risen indeed, and hath appeared to Simon.

And they told what things were done in the way, and how he was known of them in breaking of bread.

And as they thus spake, Jesus himself stood in the midst of them, and saith unto them, Peace be unto you.

But they were terrified and affrighted, and supposed that they had seen a spirit.

And he said unto them, Why are ye troubled? and why do thoughts arise in your hearts?

Behold my hands and my feet, that it is I myself: handle me, and see; for a spirit hath not flesh and bones, as ye see me have.

And when he had thus spoken, he shewed them his hands and his feet.

And while they yet believed not for joy, and wondered, he said unto them, Have ye here any meat?

And they gave him a piece of a broiled fish, and of an honeycomb.

And he took it, and did eat before them.

And he said unto them, These are the words which I spake unto you, while I was yet with you, that all things must be fulfilled, which were written in the law of Moses, and in the prophets, and in the psalms, concerning me.

Then opened he their understanding, that they might understand the scriptures,

And said unto them, Thus it is written, and thus it behooved Christ to suffer, and to rise from the dead the third day:

And that repentance and remission of sins should be preached in his name among all nations, beginning at Jerusalem.

And ye are witnesses of these things.

And, behold, I send the promise of my Father upon you: but tarry ye in the city of Jerusalem, until ye be endued with power from on high.

And he led them out as far as to Bethany, and he lifted up his hands, and blessed them.

And it came to pass, while he blessed them, he was parted from them, and carried up into heaven.

And they worshipped him, and returned to Jerusalem with great joy:

And were continually in the temple, praising and blessing God. Amen.

ONE-PAGE WITNESSING

JESUS TELLS THE WOMAN THAT HE IS CHRIST THE MESSIAH

John 4:25,26

The woman saith unto him, I know that Messias cometh, which is called Christ: when he is come, he will tell us all things.

Jesus saith unto her, I that speak unto thee am he.

ONE-PAGE WITNESSING

John 5:39-46

Search the scriptures; for in them ye think ye have eternal life: and they are they which testify of me.

And ye will not come to me, that ye might have life.

I receive not honour from men.

But I know you, that ye have not the love of God in you.

I am come in my Father's name, and ye receive me not: if another shall come in his own name, him ye will receive.

How can ye believe, which receive honour one of another, and seek not the honour that cometh from God only?

Do not think that I will accuse you to the Father: there is one that accuseth you, even Moses, in whom ye trust.

For had ye believed Moses, ye would have believed me; for he wrote of me.

ONE-PAGE WITNESSING

John 6:30-40

They said therefore unto him, What sign shewest thou then, that we may see, and believe thee? what dost thou work?

Our fathers did eat manna in the desert; as it is written, He gave them bread from heaven to eat.

Then Jesus said unto them, Verily, verily, I say unto you, Moses gave you not that bread from heaven; but my Father giveth you the true bread from heaven.

For the bread of God is he which cometh down from heaven, and giveth life unto the world.

Then said they unto him, Lord, evermore give us this bread.

And Jesus said unto them, I am the bread of life: he that cometh to me shall never hunger; and he that believeth on me shall never thirst.

But I said unto you, That ye also have seen me, and believe not.

All that the Father giveth me shall come to me; and him that cometh to me I will in no wise cast out.

For I came down from heaven, not to do mine own will, but the will of him that sent me.

Margaret F. Blanchon

And this is the Father's will which hath sent me, that of all which he hath given me I should lose nothing, but should raise it up again at the last day.

And this is the will of him that sent me, that every one which seeth the Son, and believeth on him, may have everlasting life: and I will raise him up at the last day.

ONE-PAGE WITNESSING

John 9:35-38

Jesus heard that they had cast him out; and when he had found him, he said unto him, Dost thou believe on the Son of God?

He answered and said, Who is he, Lord, that I might believe on him?

And Jesus said unto him, Thou hast both seen him, and it is he that talketh with thee.

And he said, Lord, I believe. And he worshipped him.

ONE-PAGE WITNESSING

John 11: 23-26

Jesus saith unto her, Thy brother shall rise again.

Martha saith unto him, I know that he shall rise again in the resurrection at the last day.

Jesus said unto her, I am the resurrection, and the life: he that believeth in me, though he were dead, yet shall he live:

And whosoever liveth and believeth in me shall never die. Believest thou this?

She saith unto him, Yea, Lord: I believe that thou art the Christ, the Son of God, which should come into the world.

ONE-PAGE WITNESSING

The Lord Jesus Christ's resurrection and ascension was seen by His disciples and His angels

Acts 1:1-12

The former treatise have I made, O Theophilus, of all that Jesus began both to do and teach,

Until the day in which he was taken up, after that he through the Holy Ghost had given commandments unto the apostles whom he had chosen:

To whom also he shewed himself alive after his passion by many infallible proofs, being seen of them forty days, and speaking of the things pertaining to the kingdom of God:

And, being assembled together with them, commanded them that they should not depart from Jerusalem, but wait for the promise of the Father, which, saith he, ye have heard of me.

For John truly baptized with water; but ye shall be baptized with the Holy Ghost not many days hence.

When they therefore were come together, they asked of him, saying, Lord, wilt thou at this time restore again the kingdom to Israel?

And he said unto them, It is not for you to know the times or the seasons, which the Father hath put in his own power.

But ye shall receive power, after that the Holy Ghost is come upon you: and ye shall be witnesses unto me both in Jerusalem, and in all Judaea, and in Samaria, and unto the uttermost part of the earth.

And when he had spoken these things, while they beheld, he was taken up; and a cloud received him out of their sight.

And while they looked stedfastly toward heaven as he went up, behold, two men stood by them in white apparel;

Which also said, Ye men of Galilee, why stand ye gazing up into heaven? this same Jesus, which is taken up from you into heaven, shall so come in like manner as ye have seen him go into heaven.

Then returned they unto Jerusalem from the mount called Olivet, which is from Jerusalem a sabbath day's journey.

ONE-PAGE WITNESSING

Acts 10:36-43

The word which God sent unto the children of Israel, preaching peace by Jesus Christ: (he is Lord of all:)

That word, I say, ye know, which was published throughout all Judaea, and began from Galilee, after the baptism which John preached;

How God anointed Jesus of Nazareth with the Holy Ghost and with power: who went about doing good, and healing all that were oppressed of the devil; for God was with him.

And we are witnesses of all things which he did both in the land of the Jews, and in Jerusalem; whom they slew and hanged on a tree:

Him God raised up the third day, and shewed him openly;

Not to all the people, but unto witnesses chosen before God, even to us, who did eat and drink with him after he rose from the dead.

And he commanded us to preach unto the people, and to testify that it is he which was ordained of God to be the Judge of quick and dead.

To him give all the prophets witness, that through his name whosoever believeth in him shall receive remission of sins.

ONE-PAGE WITNESSING

Acts 26:14-18

And when we were all fallen to the earth, I heard a voice speaking unto me, and saying in the Hebrew tongue, Saul, Saul, why persecutest thou me? it is hard for thee to kick against the pricks.

And I said, Who art thou, Lord? And he said, I am Jesus whom thou persecutest.

But rise, and stand upon thy feet: for I have appeared unto thee for this purpose, to make thee a minister and a witness both of these things which thou hast seen, and of those things in the which I will appear unto thee;

Delivering thee from the people, and from the Gentiles, unto whom now I send thee,

To open their eyes, and to turn them from darkness to light, and from the power of Satan unto God, that they may receive forgiveness of sins, and inheritance among them which are sanctified by faith that is in me.

ONE-PAGE WITNESSING

Psalm 22:15,16

My strength is dried up like a potsherd; and my tongue cleaveth to my jaws; and thou hast brought me into the dust of death.

For dogs have compassed me: the assembly of the wicked have inclosed me: they pierced my hands and my feet.

Zechariah 13:7

Awake, O sword, against my shepherd, and against the man that is my fellow, saith the LORD of hosts: smite the shepherd, and the sheep shall be scattered: and I will turn mine hand upon the little ones.

Zechariah 12:10

And I will pour upon the house of David, and upon the inhabitants of Jerusalem, the spirit of grace and of supplications: and they shall look upon me whom they have pierced, and they shall mourn for him, as one mourneth for his only son, and shall be in bitterness for him, as one that is in bitterness for his firstborn.

Isaiah 53:5

But he was wounded for our transgressions, he was bruised for our iniquities: the chastisement of our peace was upon him; and with his stripes we are healed.

Isaiah 53:6

All we like sheep have gone astray; we have turned every one to his own way; and the LORD hath laid on him the iniquity of us all.

ONE-PAGE WITNESSING

Daniel 9:26

And after threescore and two weeks shall Messiah be cut off, but not for himself: and the people of the prince that shall come shall destroy the city and the sanctuary; and the end thereof shall be with a flood, and unto the end of the war desolations are determined.

Luke 24:26

Ought not Christ to have suffered these things, and to enter into his glory?

Luke 24:46

And said unto them, Thus it is written, and thus it behooved Christ to suffer, and to rise from the dead the third day:

1 Peter 1:11

Searching what, or what manner of time the Spirit of Christ which was in them did signify, when it testified beforehand the sufferings of Christ, and the glory that should follow.

1 Peter 2:24

Who his own self bare our sins in his own body on the tree, that we, being dead to sins, should live unto righteousness: by whose stripes ye were healed.

ONE-PAGE WITNESSING

Psalm 16:10

For thou wilt not leave my soul in hell; neither wilt thou suffer thine Holy One to see corruption.

Isaiah 53:10

Yet it pleased the LORD to bruise him; he hath put him to grief: when thou shalt make his soul an offering for sin, he shall see his seed, he shall prolong his days, and the pleasure of the LORD shall prosper in his hand.

Hosea 6:2

After two days will he revive us: in the third day he will raise us up, and we shall live in his sight.

Acts 2:25

For David speaketh concerning him, I foresaw the Lord always before my face, for he is on my right hand, that I should not be moved:

ONE-PAGE WITNESSING

Colossians 1:12-20

Giving thanks unto the Father, which hath made us meet to be partakers of the inheritance of the saints in light:

Who hath delivered us from the power of darkness, and hath translated us into the kingdom of his dear Son:

In whom we have redemption through his blood, even the forgiveness of sins:

Who is the image of the invisible God, the firstborn of every creature:

For by him were all things created, that are in heaven, and that are in earth, visible and invisible, whether they be thrones, or dominions, or principalities, or powers: all things were created by him, and for him:

And he is before all things, and by him all things consist.

And he is the head of the body, the church: who is the beginning, the firstborn from the dead; that in all things he might have the preeminence.

For it pleased the Father that in him should all fulness dwell;

And, having made peace through the blood of his cross, by him to reconcile all things unto himself; by him, I say, whether they be things in earth, or things in heaven.

ONE-PAGE WITNESSING

1 Timothy 6:15,16

Which in his times he shall shew, who is the blessed and only Potentate, the King of kings, and Lord of lords;

Who only hath immortality, dwelling in the light which no man can approach unto; whom no man hath seen, nor can see: to whom be honour and power everlasting. Amen.

ONE-PAGE WITNESSING

Titus 3:4,5

> *But after that the kindness and love of God our Saviour toward man appeared,*

> *Not by works of righteousness which we have done, but according to his mercy he saved us, by the washing of regeneration, and renewing of the Holy Ghost;*

ONE-PAGE WITNESSING

Hebrews 1:1-3

God, who at sundry times and in divers manners spake in time past unto the fathers by the prophets,

Hath in these last days spoken unto us by his Son, whom he hath appointed heir of all things, by whom also he made the worlds;

Who being the brightness of his glory, and the express image of his person,

and upholding all things by the word of his power, when he had by himself purged our sins, sat down on the right hand of the Majesty on high:

ONE-PAGE WITNESSING

1 Peter 1:18

Forasmuch as ye know that ye were not redeemed with corruptible things, as silver and gold, from your vain conversation received by tradition from your fathers;

ONE-PAGE WITNESSING

2 Peter 1:16-21

For we have not followed cunningly devised fables, when we made known unto you the power and coming of our Lord Jesus Christ, but were eyewitnesses of his majesty.

For he received from God the Father honour and glory, when there came such a voice to him from the excellent glory, This is my beloved Son, in whom I am well pleased.

And this voice which came from heaven we heard, when we were with him in the holy mount.

We have also a more sure word of prophecy; whereunto ye do well that ye take heed, as unto a light that shineth in a dark place, until the day dawn, and the day star arise in your hearts:

Knowing this first, that no prophecy of the scripture is of any private interpretation.

For the prophecy came not in old time by the will of man: but holy men of God spake as they were moved by the Holy Ghost.

SCRIPTURES referring to

THE POWER OF THE PRECIOUS BLOOD OF OUR LORD AND SAVIOUR JESUS CHRIST

BLOOD SCRIPTURES

Leviticus 17:11

> *The Blood is an atonement for our soul. Without the shedding of blood there is no forgiveness*

Matthew 26:28

> *For this is My Blood of the New Testament*

Mark 14:24

> *And he said unto them, This is my blood of the new testament which is shed for many.*

Luke 22:20

> *Likewise also the cup after supper, saying, This cup is the new testament in my blood, which is shed for you.*

Acts 13:27-39

> *For they that dwell at Jerusalem, and their rulers, because they knew him not, nor yet the voices of the prophets which are read every Sabbath day, they have fulfilled them in condemning him.*

> *And though they found no cause of death in him, yet desired they Pilate that he should be slain.*

Acts 20:28

feed the church of God which He has purchased with His Own Blood.

1 Corinthians 11:25

After the same manner also he took the cup, when he had supped saying, This cup is the new testament in my blood: this do ye; as oft as ye drink it in remembrance of me.

Ephesians 1:7

In whom we have redemption through his blood, the forgiveness of sins, according to the riches of his grace;

Hebrews 9:12

By His own Blood He entered into the Most Holy Place, having obtained eternal forgiveness for us

v.14

How much more shall the blood of Christ, who through the eternal Spirit offered himself without spot to God, purge your conscience from dead works to serve the living God

v.22

And almost all things are by the law purged with blood; and without shedding of blood is no remission.

v.24

For Christ is not entered into the holy places made with hands, which are the figures of the true; but into heaven itself, now to appear in the presence of God for us

v.26

For then must he often have suffered since the foundation of the world: but now once in the end of the world hath he appeared to put away sin by the sacrifice of himself.

v.28

So Christ was once offered to bear the sins of many; and unto them that look for him shall he appear the second time without sin unto salvation.

Hebrews 10:5,6

Wherefore when he comes into the world, he says, "Sacrifice and offering thou wouldest not, but a body hast thou prepared me: in burnt offerings and sacrifices for sin thou hast had no pleasure.

v.7

Then said I, Lo, I come (in the volume of the book it is written of me) to do thy will, O God.

v.9,10

Then said he, Lo, I come to do thy will, O God. He takes away the first, that he may establish the second. By the which will we are sanctified through the offering of the body of Jesus Christ once for all.

v.12

> But this man, after he had offered one sacrifice for sins forever, sat down on the right hand of God.

v.14

> For by one offering he has perfected forever them that are sanctified.

v.29

> …and has counted the blood of the covenant, wherewith he was <u>sanctified</u> …

Hebrews 13:12

> Wherefore Jesus also, that He might sanctify the people with His own Blood suffered without the gate.

Hebrews 13:20

> Now the God of peace, that brought again from the dead our Lord Jesus, that great shepherd of the sheep, <u>through the blood of the everlasting covenant</u>, make you perfect in every good work to do His will, working in you that which is well pleasing in his sight, through Jesus Christ; to whom be glory forever and ever. Amen.…

1 John 1:7-9

> But if we walk in the light, as he is in the light, we have fellowship one with another, and the blood of Jesus Christ his Son cleanses us from all sin.

1 John 5: 6-8

This is he that came by water and blood, even Jesus Christ; not by water only, but by water and blood. And it is the Spirit that beareth witness, because the Spirit is truth.

For there are three that bear record in heaven, the Father, the Word, and the Holy Ghost: and these three are one.

And there are three that bear witness in earth, the Spirit, and the water, and the blood: and these three agree in one.

Revelation 1:5

Unto Him that Loved us, and washed us from our sins in His own Blood.